"I was concerned at first that this was going t
au contraire! Dr. Amy artfully weaves solid re
need for self-awareness, understanding, com,   empathy –
all pointed to improving my ability to lead and connect in today's world.
And I love her personal stories. They provide concrete examples and
techniques on ways to open dialogue and become a better person,
leader, husband and community-builder."

–STEVE RASCHE
Chief Financial Officer and Executive Vice President
Spire

"Dr. Narishkin's *The Communication Connection* is grounded in science
but not unnecessarily academic. Her book is compassionate without
being saccharine. Above all, it is practical, with real-life exercises and
experiments. This is a great book for anyone who wants to engage their
staff or anyone, in more human connections and conversation."

–TERENCE BOSTIC, PH.D
Managing Partner
CMA Global

"Dr. Amy Narishkin's book is a masterful synthesis of profound
theoretical insights and practical advice drawn from professional
and personal experiences with her clients and friends. This book goes
beyond highlighting the economic, moral and psychological benefits
of embracing differences. It offers thoughtful, actionable strategies
for navigating diversity while maintaining personal well-being.
Dr. Narishkin draws from the rich framework of cultural intelligence
to explain essential skills: listening, slowing down, building connections,
and ultimately, collaborating effectively in diverse environments.
Slow down, please, and read this excellent guide. I loved it and
recommend it wholeheartedly."

–PIOTR PERCZYŃSKI, PH.D
Professor
Leiden University and Webster University, Leiden campus, the Netherlands

"*The Communication Connection* is an invaluable resource for leaders and individuals who want to develop an inclusive culture within their organisations and communities. Dr. Narishkin's decades of research are evident in her knowledge of the intricacies of cultural intelligence and effective communication.

Her insights are not just theoretical; they are grounded in real-world applications and case studies. Her storytelling is compelling and educational; her approach is compassionate and pragmatic; and her writing is clear and accessible—all contributing to an effective roadmap to navigate the complexities of cultural differences. *The Communication Connection* is a must-read for leaders, educators and individuals alike."

—VIPUL VACHHANI
CEO
Jaivel, United Kingdom and India

"There couldn't be a better time for Dr. Amy Narishkin's book. Daily news reminds us of the necessity to reach across cultures to achieve shared objectives in a shattering world. As Dr. Narishkin practically explains, cultural intelligence is the key to the understanding and fruitful cooperation we need!"

—ALAIN SIX
Founder
Green Wave Investments, France

"*The Communication Connection* is an indispensable tool in the war for talent. This book's riveting case studies and practical tactics will transform recruiting and retention for your company."

—DAVID WALTERS
CEO
Hy-C Company

"Dr. Amy Narishkin offers a heartfelt, practical guide to fostering genuine human connections in workplaces and communities – one meaningful conversation at a time. Through relatable stories and real-world examples, Amy demonstrates how essential it is to slow down, acknowledge assumptions and prioritize listening and learning. She empowers readers to confidently navigate diversity, foster inclusion and cultivate a cohesive culture. *The Communication Connection* is indispensable for leaders, educators and anyone committed to creating environments where people feel valued, heard, seen and engaged."

—GREG ATCHISON, PH.D.
Principal Chair
C12 of Greater St. Louis

"This practical and straightforward book provides tools and strategies, backed by research, to apply what you learn, strengthen your personal growth, and inspire positive change in your everyday interactions. The real-world case studies and 5 C's help navigate culture, assumption, bias, compassion, trust and listening for a shared understanding of people with perspectives and backgrounds different than your own."

—LORI DRURY
Executive Director and CEO
Biblical Business Training

"*The Communication Connection* is a must-have for leaders who truly want to be effective communicators across a spectrum of employees, customers and other stakeholders. Dr. Amy Narishkin provides concepts and tools for anyone to understand cultural intelligence, be cognizant of your pre-existing thoughts and actions, and effectively create and expand relationships with anyone. It is a treasure chest of knowledge and ideas."

—GREG MEIER
President and CEO
Peak Performance

"Dr. Amy Narishkin takes us on an insightful, reflective journey through cultural intelligence by offering practical tools to navigate challenging conversations. *The Communication Connection* shows us how to lean into compassion, cultivate understanding and foster positive interactions in an increasingly interconnected world."

–JENNIFER MORALES
Insurance Consultant

"Dr. Amy Narishkin's book is a timely guide to navigating cultural differences and overcoming preconceptions. I found it valuable with its real-life examples of interactions that have gone well and others that have not gone so well. Dr. Narishkin gives specific steps to bridge our differences and help us see eye-to-eye, or at least to understand another's point of view, even when we may not understand exactly where they are coming from. Being the boss doesn't make you a good manager; it's tools like the ones you find in this book that make you a good manager."

–MIKE COOP
Chief Financial Officer
Laclede Chain Manufacturing

"*The Communication Connection* is a great read, especially for those who want to have impactful relationships, professionally and personally. Dr. Amy thoroughly teaches and guides you on how to make genuine human connections by consistently applying cultural intelligence. She knows her stuff! This is a book you'll reference time and time again!"

–GWEN DOSS
Chief Engineer
Boeing

"I had the wonderful opportunity to participate in Dr. Amy Narishkin's cultural intelligence training a few years ago. I'm thrilled that she has now written *The Communication Connection* so I can revisit case studies, quotes, references and personal stories. So timely once again!"

–DOREEN BARTOLDUS
Former President, National Association of Women in Construction
Senior Director, Brown & Caldwell

"Dr. Amy Narishkin left no stone unturned in *The Communication Connection*. The book is a thorough guide to navigating uncertainty in the workplace. Each chapter offers a carefully designed plan that, if followed, will lead to an organization that honors and respects a diverse workforce. It all begins with the admonition to slow down, listen and seek to see the ways we all belong. Compassion is at the heart of this book."

—KAREN CASEY, PHD
President and CEO
Karen Casey Publishing
www.womens-spirituality.com

"A more than helpful read to move any organization or business toward a healthier corporate culture. We're all aware that our workforce is the key to success. The information and steps in this book will move any organization to retain the best workforce possible."

—WAYNE CRULL
Managing Partner
WD 60

"This book shows readers how to see, model and experience the dignity and innate worth of all human beings, which results in effective communication, great relationships and successful businesses. *The Communication Connection* includes practical tools, opportunities for practice and lots of up-close examples of people who learn their way to great outcomes. It will help you get to the deeply satisfying outcomes you're looking for, too."

—ANNE COLLIER
Executive Director
The Net Safety Collaborative

"*The Communication Connection*" offers vital tools for today's chaotic world. Dr. Narishkin's case studies are captivating, practical and down-to-earth. This book will help you and your organization in any country resolve people problems across gender, generations, nationality and socio-economic differences."

—MARGARITA ZAPIAIN
PhD candidate, Head of Language Department
Escuela Normal Superior Federal de Aguascalientes, Mexico

THE
COMMUNICATION
CONNECTION

Confidently Create a Cohesive Culture
One Conversation at a Time

AMY NARISHKIN, PHD

The Communication Connection
Confidently Create a Cohesive Culture, One Conversation at a Time
Amy Narishkin, PhD

Published by Empowering Leaders Press, St. Louis, Missouri, USA

Project Management and Book Design:
Davis Creative, LLC, dba: DavisCreativePublishing.com

Library of Congress Cataloging-in-Publication Data
Names: Narishkin, Amy, author.
Title: The communication connection : confidently create a cohesive culture one conversation at a time / Amy Narishkin, PhD.
Description: St. Louis, MO : Empowering Leaders Press, [2025] | Includes bibliographical references.
Identifiers: ISBN: 979-8-9926859-0-9 (paperback) | 979-8-9926859-1-6 (ebook) | LCCN: 2025903261
Subjects: LCSH: Communication in organizations. | Interpersonal communication. | Corporate culture. | Industrial relations. | Cultural awareness. | BISAC: BUSINESS & ECONOMICS / Organizational Development. | BUSINESS & ECONOMICS / Human Resources & Personnel Management. | BUS118000 BUSINESS & ECONOMICS / Diversity & Inclusion.
Classification: LCC: HD30.3 .N37 2025 | DDC: 658.45--dc23

ATTENTION CORPORATIONS, UNIVERSITIES, COLLEGES, AND PROFESSIONAL ORGANIZATIONS: Quantity discounts are available on bulk purchases of this book for educational, gift purposes, or as premiums for increasing magazine subscriptions or renewals. Special books or book excerpts can also be created to fit specific needs. For information, please contact Empowering Leaders Press, Info@EmpoweringPartners.com.

EMPOWERING
— PARTNERS —

EmpoweringPartners.com

DEDICATION

This book is dedicated to readers who don't want to inadvertently minimize the human element of their organization or community. They recognize that when people are the priority, there's more engagement, collaboration, productivity and commitment in any organization. They've discovered they need to practice regular self-care so that they have the bandwidth to slow down, hear people out and learn about and from them. They want to grow and learn, check the impact of their words and actions and are willing to pivot to improve the quality of their encounters. They do this because they are wise, big-hearted people who know any sustainable organization has a cohesive culture that is built one conversation at a time.

TABLE OF CONTENTS

FOREWORD

I have known Dr. Amy Narishkin since we met during our doctoral studies at the University of Missouri-St. Louis. Since then, I have had the honor of seeing her develop a business that touches the soul of organizations by helping individuals be fully present in their work, thus improving performance, engagement, and commitment.

Dr. Narishkin – better known as "Dr. Amy" – and I became friends, colleagues, and difference-makers when we facilitated seminars together to initiate "sticky" and uncomfortable discussions about race relations, cultural differences and religion. Our audiences for over three years were Black and White groups of adults from distinct areas of our city, sprinkled with urban high school students, and clergy personnel from other churches. These life-changing, mind-awakening sessions took place in our small church located in a predominately Black neighborhood on the North side of our city – St. Louis.

Our seminars and workshops were during the height of the Michael Brown protests in Ferguson, Missouri, a time when our city erupted with marches, riots, military personnel, and chaos in the streets. This tragedy garnered national and international attention. It also brought Dr. Amy and me together to form a unique tag team motivated by our humanitarian hearts for our community.

I admit, as a Black man who experienced the segregated and desegregated South in the '60s and '70s, I never would have dreamed, imagined, had the tolerance for, nor openly sought to be in a partnership with a White female whose life and experiences were cultivated within a majority culture with opportunities so different from my own. But Dr. Amy persevered and stuck with me as I came to open my mind and heart. Her genuine care, authenticity, and desire to learn immediately came through, erasing my skepticism and building trust and collaboration.

Today, Dr. Amy uses these same skills and learnings to help leaders build diverse, unified, collaborative teams that cause organizations to thrive. Her expertise and passion are on full display in her new book *The Communication Connection: Confidently Create a Cohesive Culture One Conversation at a Time*. Dr. Amy has done a fantastic job in this literary work that you are about to absorb. You, as a reader and lifelong learner, will greatly benefit from being introduced to the 5 C's of culture intelligence and discovering ways to develop meaningful and professional connections, even when engaging in unfamiliar territories. Whether you're an employee, employer, administrator, or CEO, *The Communication Connection* will easily become one of your favorite go-to resources.

I salute the prowess, courageous heart, and quality leadership of Dr. Amy Narishkin in her unwavering efforts to make a meaningful difference among people from all walks of life by using the most powerful means that all cultures and humanity can identify: the art and science of communication.

Dr. Julius R. Sims
Consultant/Pastor/Teacher

INTRODUCTION

I live in St. Louis, Missouri. Though significant for so many reasons, the city is particularly important for me because it's ground zero for the latest Civil Rights movement.

What ignited the movement was Michael Brown's death in Ferguson, Missouri on August 8, 2014. Ferguson is one of 72 townships in the St. Louis metro area, just 20 minutes north of my township.

But I wasn't in town when Michael died. Our family was in France with 25 of my husband, Cyril's cousins, celebrating the 75th anniversary of D-day. Cyril's grandfather had been a part of the French Resistance during World War II. In 1944, his grandfather rode his bike to the Normandy coast. He had been called up to meet the Allied troops to which he was assigned to escort, translate and fight alongside as they strove to take back France from the occupying Nazi forces. Cyril and I, plus our four children ages 12-22 at the time, spent a week with the cousins reenacting our grandfather's 235-mile bike ride from Paris to Granville, Normandy. It was a challenging bike ride for our family – physically, emotionally and spiritually – recognizing the sacrifices people made and reliving painful collective memories the war had left behind. Being so focused on our family's journey, I was oblivious to what was happening here at home in St. Louis.

I was oblivious, that is, until we returned home to St. Louis and a fellow parent at our kids' school asked me what I thought about Ferguson. Until that time, I didn't know anything in particular was happening. I didn't realize anything was happening because of where we live in St. Louis. Where we live, there was no unrest. And no one was talking about the protesting-by-day and rioting-by-night in Ferguson.

Then, just as I dug into the news, we heard from family in France that Ferguson was front-page news in Paris. Our French cousins messaged us to see if we were okay. Oddly enough, though our family and friends across the ocean were talking about it, no one in our town just 20 minutes from Ferguson was talking about the events. The silence around us was deafening.

When I asked my kids about how they were talking about Ferguson in school, I learned they weren't. The subject was off-limits. When I looked into it, I learned there was a gag order over many schools in the St. Louis metro area.

Similarly, if I brought up the topic with people around me, folks looked awkward and would change the subject. But avoiding tough topics was not how I was raised. Back in his day, my dad had been the CEO of two multinational Fortune 500 companies. He got to know people by engaging them in hearty discussions. Since childhood, I watched how he'd lean into conversations by letting the other person lead. He'd listen for a point with which he could connect and center the conversation on them. His approach of being a learner and listener allowed him to feel comfortable talking with just about anyone. It showed me at a young age, people are worthy of dignity and it's on me to learn their story. Now I work with organizations and their leaders who want to be confident communicators so they can create a cohesive culture in their organization, one conversation at a time.

Sadly, my dad is long gone. But I get to operationalize his legacy by practicing and teaching cultural intelligence – compassion for a person within their unique context – in organizations and communities. I get to carry forward what he modeled by leaning into challenging conversations, listening to understand and uncovering a way to connect with each person and organization I encounter.

So, when no one within my White community would talk with me about what was going on in Ferguson, I searched for someone who would. I reached out to a Black colleague of mine from my doctoral program at the University of Missouri-St. Louis, Pastor Dr. Julius Sims.

Pastor Julius and I realized that as educators, we could work with people and help get the conversation started. So we started cross-race conversations in his Black church in north St. Louis City.

As Pastor Julius and I were facilitating these, what Pastor called, "Courageous Conversations," I was learning too. I discovered many people had not had an upbringing like mine. Blacks and Whites did not necessarily know how to engage in such challenging conversations. In fact, some people felt ashamed they didn't have the vocabulary or skills to talk with someone who has a different perspective and background.

More to learn

Though I had some exposure and skills for talking with people who have different perspectives and backgrounds, it did not mean I didn't have a lot more to learn. A lot of what I learned initially came by participating and eventually joining Pastor Julius' congregation. I remember well an event early on where I felt particularly awkward.

Awkward was certainly the way I felt when we arrived at the church fair on that late August day. It was already sweltering at 9 am. That morning, the Word of Life Christian Church in North City St. Louis was hosting their annual church fair and school supply giveaway event. The event was being held across the street from our pocket-sized church on a rugged parking lot that sat in the shadow of a three-story abandoned school building.

When my husband, Cyril, and I arrived, our fellow church members were in full swing, setting up chairs, tables, grills and tents. After we greeted and hugged everyone, Cyril jumped right in and got to work helping with setup. He's more extroverted than I am; I'm more reserved and thoughtful. With all the hustle and bustle, all I could do was stand there in the middle of the parking lot wondering, "What can I, a White woman in an all-Black neighborhood, possibly have to offer?" Sure, I was a member of the church, but not everybody at this event was a member or even knew me.

In that quiet moment, it occurred to me that whatever I did, it would be good to sit down and not stand over people. I thought to myself, "That's a good idea... OK, but where?"

That's when I saw my buddy Jonathan at the entrance acting as a one-man welcoming committee. He was standing by a card table with two chairs provided for visitors to sit down and complete a short questionnaire. I thought, "That's where I can sit."

I went over, sat down and watched how Jonathan so easily engaged with folks, clapping shoulders and shaking hands. He knew the language of the community and shared their skin color. Since Jonathan and I often chat it up, it felt natural to help him with greeting. So, I stayed there, seated at the table. It wasn't long before I noticed fellow moms, who had come for the school supplies, joining me at the table to complete the questionnaire.

Sitting there, I first noticed I was at kid eye level. I got to talk with the children, share my name and ask them theirs. The little ones would tell me about their teacher and give me a hug. The teens would chat with me and laugh about their experiences. It was pretty clear the most important thing for me to do was lean in, deeply listen and appreciate their experience.

Assumptions left at the gate

Since the first day of school had been three days earlier, I asked one little girl how school was going. As an educator, I'd heard that kids in the city don't always start school the first day, but I didn't know why. That didn't seem right since kids would start off the year already behind. But that day at the card table, I decided to leave my assumptions at the gate and just learn.

The little girl said she hadn't started school yet. Her mom, who was sitting with me at the table, looked up and told me she'd lost her job as a nursing assistant. She didn't have the money for her daughter's school uniform.

For just a moment, I was quiet and then said, "I get it. I'd want my child prepared for school." The girl's mom visibly relaxed. Jonathan overheard the conversation and offered to connect her with a friend who's a nurse to see if she could help her find a job. I asked, "May I make a suggestion?" She nodded. I said, "If you'd like help getting a uniform, perhaps you can ask the ladies in the church." She gave us each a hug and headed over to church.

At first, my sitting there at the table seemed insignificant, but I began to see its value. Just sitting there communicated: "I'm listening up – not down – to you," and we're in no rush. You matter. I could also see the impact of waiting and allowing people to reveal themselves, their needs, in their time.

More to the story

Another mom came in through the gate with her three teenage children, a son and two daughters. When the mom sat down with the questionnaire, her daughters launched into telling me all about school. As we chatted, I noticed their brother was quiet, rather stoic. I asked him, "How's school going?" He looked down and quietly shook his head. Their mom looked up and said, "He hasn't started yet. He has developmental delays. I'm worried he'll be bullied. I haven't been able to get off work to meet with his teachers."

I reflected on my own experience for just a moment and then said, "I understand; we need our kids safe. I've got children with learning disabilities. I like to meet with their teachers too. Do you mind if I ask you a question?" She said it was OK. I asked, "Does your son have an

Individualized Education Plan or IEP?" She nodded. I said, "With an IEP, you can ask to meet with his team of teachers before the school year starts, when you're free."

She said, "I didn't know. I appreciate that information."

I turned to her son and said, "That's got to be tough when you don't know what the other kids are up to." He nodded. "You know, you can ask your teachers to help you figure out if a kid really wants to be your friend or if they're just yanking your chain. Most teachers really want to help."

He looked up at me, in the eyes, and smiled. He said, "Thank you, ma'am."

Steps for connection

That day it became very apparent that if I was going to connect in a way that was meaningful for both them and me, I had to let them lead. This was particularly true in this context. I'm a person who is White, from a historically more powerful cultural group, attempting to connect with a person who is Black, from a historically marginalized group, so I need to let them take the lead. That way they can reveal in their time and in their way what and if they want to share. This is the case for anyone in a more powerful position – whether a man talking with a woman, an adult talking with a child or a boss talking with their subordinate.

When a culturally intelligent person finds themselves in a situation where their color, gender, generation, nationality, orientation, disability or job puts them in a more powerful position, they need to double their efforts to prove they're trustworthy. This is because it isn't just them talking; rather, it's them with all their history behind them that's talking too.

To lean in and learn a person's story, take three steps:

1. Slow down, take a breath and withhold your assumption.
2. Share one short thing about yourself to show your humanity; then ask about them, listening to learn.
3. Ask if you can ask a question; don't assume it's okay to ask.

Then lean in and listen to learn. When you affirm their experience, even if it's different from your own, you create genuine human connection, along with more commitment and productivity in your organization.

CULTURAL INTELLIGENCE TOOL

To learn about another person:

1. Slow down
2. Share one short thing about yourself
3. Ask if you can ask a question

CHAPTER 1:
UNDERSTANDING CULTURAL INTELLIGENCE

*Empowering those around you to be heard and valued
makes the difference between a leader who simply
instructs and one who inspires.*

-ADENA FRIEDMAN

We've all experienced that awkward moment at one time or another. It's that moment when you or someone you know feels tongue-tied talking with a person of a different race or culture. Our common knee-jerk reaction is to minimize or not even acknowledge differences. It may seem like a good idea to go along to get along but it actually undermines people, our relationships and our enjoyment and effectiveness at work. Minimizing differences actually increases the drama and decreases productivity in most organizations and communities.

What if you could build a skill set to effectively talk and work with just about anyone? Using this skill set, called cultural intelligence, allows you and those you talk with to feel valued, heard, seen and engaged, and to be more committed and collaborative. These are the skills and tools anyone with curiosity, compassion and tenacity can develop over time.

With cultural intelligence, you'll be equipped to upend distracting day-to-day friction, collaborate within multicultural teams and create meaningful cross-cultural products and services.

Consider this: only about half of employees feel valued at work (Calvin, 2023). And considering work is where employees spend a bulk of their time, the overall feeling they have about their jobs is incredibly important to productivity, engagement, and, ultimately, success for any organization and community. So, let's unpack the question: How do you talk with people so that they feel valued, heard, seen and engaged?

Ensuring everyone feels valued, heard, seen and engaged can be tough, particularly with workplaces and communities growing more diverse by the day. So, what if you:

1. Are unsure how to navigate cross-cultural relationships?
2. Wonder if diversity in an organization just adds more conflict?
3. Say something that's hurtful?

Those are legitimate questions. In a time of uncertainty, normal responses are to shy away and remain silent, or find someone to blame and lash out in anger. Silence and violence are convenient ways to make meaning out of a bewildering situation. But another possible response to the uncertainty is empathy. Empathy is akin to solidarity, born of the understanding that we are all in this together.

In what together? For starters, we're all in the uncertainty together. And that may be exactly why you're reading this book – because you don't always know how to communicate solidarity and create connections with people who have a different perspective or background. You're not alone.

Whether it's in your community making new friends or on a conference call with colleagues, cultural intelligence enables you to create the connection that builds collaboration, engagement and commitment. **Cultural intelligence** is the ability to appreciate another person's perspective and adapt your words and actions to show genuine respect and interest in them. Put another way, you'll be able to demonstrate meaningful compassion as you learn more about the other person's context. This is cultural intelligence in action.

In this book, you'll develop the cultural intelligence skills to feel confident talking and working with just about anyone. To illustrate, I'll share stories I've gathered talking with leaders and those I've written based on executive coaching conversations with other leaders.

In many cases, leaders wonder, "Why don't I feel confident talking with people who are different?" These are common concerns I hear:

- "I may say the wrong thing."
- "I don't know what to say."
- "I might upset the person."
- "We may not have anything in common."
- "It feels awkward."

If it's awkward for the leader, imagine the impact on an entire organization. As you read these seven symptoms, see if you recognize any that are present in your organization or community. An organization lacks cultural intelligence if they intentionally or inadvertently:

1. Exclude colleagues and clients with words and actions.
2. Stifle or avoid conversations.
3. Encounter infighting between people, groups or departments.
4. Are unaware of their impact on others.
5. Fail to attract, retain and promote diverse talent.
6. Suppress the ability to reach new markets.
7. Struggle with employee engagement, commitment and turnover.

When these symptoms are present, your organization or community may not have realized yet that a cohesive culture is built one conversation at a time. Cultural intelligence is what empowers you to successfully navigate conversations with people who have a unique background or perspective so that both you and they walk away from the encounter feeling valued, heard, seen and engaged. A win-win scenario like this is cultural intelligence in action.

THE 5 C'S™ OF CULTURAL INTELLIGENCE

Cultural intelligence, in its most basic form, requires curiosity, contemplation, courage, context and compassion.

Knowing, practicing and using these five elements will grow your cultural intelligence and help you speak authentically with just about anyone.

CULTURAL INTELLIGENCE TOOL

To successfully navigate cross-cultural conversations you'll need the 5 C's™ of cultural intelligence:

1. **CURIOSITY** – the interest, intrigue and wonder about people, places and systems that are new and different, even though it may initially feel awkward, scary or hard. But curiosity alone isn't enough; you'll also need...

2. **CONTEMPLATION** – the intention of slowing down and softening your gaze to practice presence. Presence is the embodied awareness of your mental, emotional and sensory experience. With contemplation, you'll find...

3. **COURAGE** – the head and heart to pursue another even though it may initially feel awkward, scary or hard. With courage, you can discover the...

4. **CONTEXT** – the unique circumstances, history and experiences within which you live, work and play. When you come to deeply appreciate the context of another, you discover...

5. **COMPASSION** – what happens when you hold judgment a little more lightly, make room for another's perspective and feel with them. Then, in solidarity, you can create genuine connection and take meaningful action.

The following case study illustrates the power of the 5 C's™.

CASE STUDY:

CONNECTION, NOT CORRECTION

In his executive coaching session, Ralph told me when he first saw the email he immediately wondered, "What did we do wrong this time?"

Because of his position as Vice President of Operations for his hospital group, Ralph is copied on email complaints directed toward various departments, in this case, Marketing.

In this email, a Black doctor on staff expressed frustration about a billboard depicting just one White doctor, which he said suggested a different reality than the diversity their hospital group employs.

Ralph, who is White, told me he understood why this doctor was frustrated. It has to be tough not to see yourself reflected in marketing materials. He also wondered if the doctor realized they had other billboards that included their doctors of color, and he wanted to point that out to him – in effect, correct him.

I said, "That's a conundrum. What prompted you to call me?"

Ralph said, "I'm not sure how to respond to the doctor. He's a great doctor, and I don't want to inadvertently alienate him. Do I say, 'I understand your perspective, but here's the rest of the story?'"

I said, "First of all, I appreciate two things. You slowed down enough to call and think through your response with me. Also, you're already feeling for him. That's two-thirds of the problem solved right there. The trick is not just saying you understand his perspective but seeking to understand. With cultural intelligence, the goal is to get to a shared understanding with the other person; that's how you'll create a connection."

Ralph said, "Good point. What does that sound like?"

I said, "You can say what you said to me. 'It sounds like you're frustrated with Marketing. It seems like they're not acknowledging your experience in their marketing materials. That's gotta be tough.' Then drop into silence," I suggested. "Because this affirms his feelings and experience, see if he'd be willing to share more about what it's like for him.

"If you keep the conversation about him, rather than trying to correct him or change his mind, you'll understand more about his reality."

Ralph said, "It would be a lot easier if he just understood my perspective."

I said, "Absolutely, it would be easier, in the short term. But in the long run, it's opportunities like these that allow you and your leadership team to bring down barriers of communication within the whole hospital group. This is why we're partners in this work."

Ralph said, "That makes sense. I'll give it a shot and circle back with you."

I didn't hear back from Ralph. Then at lunchtime he texted me to say, "The conversation went well. Thanks, Dr. Amy." I thought we were all set. Then right on the heels of that text came another one. Ralph said, "At least the conversation went well for me, but I'm not sure how it impacted the doctor."

Ralph was totally catching on; he understood his impact may be different than his intent. I called him right away and said, "You're nailing it. This is the perfect time to lean in, show your genuine concern and seek understanding."

Ralph said, "Really? What does that sound like?"

I said, "It sounds like just what you said to me, 'That conversation went well for me, but what was the impact on you?'" Ralph agreed to call the doctor back.

What happened

I didn't hear back from Ralph immediately. But then, on his commute home, he called me. Ralph told me he reached out to the doctor to check his impact. That's when the doctor opened up and explained how he felt sidelined a number of times over the last few months; the billboard with the single White doctor was the final straw. The doctor shared how he completed extra work in medical school to develop his specialty area and how the billboard made him think he and his work weren't worth the trouble.

Ralph told me he really felt for the doctor and told him so. He let the doctor know he didn't need to bury his hurt anymore; he should let him know any time there's a concern. The doctor told Ralph how much he appreciated him following up and showing his concern.

With a genuine connection made, Ralph told me that's when he realized he could let the doctor know there are other billboards depicting doctors and nurses of color, representing the diversity the hospital group employs. So, he suggested to the doctor that he doesn't actually think this is an external marketing problem but an internal one because the doctor didn't know. Ralph asked the doctor if they could talk with the marketing department together and ask them to do a better job of letting staff know about their plans. The doctor appreciated the offer and accepted it.

Ralph said, "I get it. Now I understand what you mean by seeking to understand so that the doctor and I could come to a shared understanding and mutual respect."

I said, "You nailed it. That win-win scenario you created is cultural intelligence in action. With what took a total of 15 minutes of your day, you helped create a more cohesive culture within your hospital group. The compassion you expressed for his context also has a ripple effect throughout the organization. Feeling valued, heard, seen and engaged, the doctor will now help to create better patient outcomes too."

Ralph said, "That's true. Thank you!"

Ralph's 5 C's™

Curiosity – Ralph was curious about the doctor's complaint, wondered if the doctor knew there were other billboards and thought about calling me for input.

Contemplation – Instead of rushing in to correct the doctor, Ralph slowed down and got contemplative. He took time to consider the doctor's complaint, his own feelings and how to approach the doctor with genuine care and respect.

Courage – It would've been easier in the short term for Ralph to just send an email explaining about the other billboards. Instead, Ralph was courageous; he asked for my help and then sought out the doctor to learn more. It took courage to downshift from being the leader with all the answers to being a servant leader who was ready to learn and connect.

Context – Ralph took the time to hear the doctor out and learn about his experience. This effort provided Ralph with the context he needed to demonstrate compassion in a way that was meaningful for the doctor.

Compassion – After the first call, Ralph wondered about his impact, prompting him to call a second time for more clarity and understanding. This compassionate action led to a more authentic personal relationship and effective professional relationship. The doctor felt valued, heard, seen and engaged.

Like Ralph, utilizing the 5 C's™, you can practice your cultural intelligence. But whether you're a vice president, CEO, head of human resources, executive director, community leader or a person who wants to see less polarization at work and in the world, these tools can help you:

1. Talk and work with just about anyone.
2. Discover how assumptions block genuine conversations.
3. See both similarities and differences as valuable for building relationships, collaboration, productivity and commitment.

4. Acknowledge and utilize your feelings as a guide through awkward conversations.

5. Demonstrate that you are a learner and have a growth mindset.

6. Appreciate a different perspective and offer your own so that you both walk away feeling valued, heard, seen and engaged.

7. Be more genuine at work, in your community and at home.

8. Slow down to work fast and effectively.

9. Recognize the value of giving and receiving compassion.

10. Collaborate with other people even when there are great differences.

11. Discover how to bridge gaps and avoid "us versus them" traps.

12. Successfully create a win-win scenario in your conversations.

13. Cultivate allies and be a better advocate.

14. Be more likeable.

15. Feel confident about leading and working with a diverse team.

VALUE OF JOURNALING

Cultural intelligence isn't something you just have; it's something you develop over a lifetime. And since cultural intelligence is developed one conversation at a time, journaling allows you to reflect on and learn from your encounters. That reflection process can be as powerful, if not more powerful, than the actual conversation itself. Journaling also provides you with a dated record of progress, setbacks and successes so that dots can be connected, patterns can be noticed, and you and others can be recognized for helping to create a more cohesive and compassionate culture at work, in your community and at home.

Journaling your insights, reflections and questions also develops your self-awareness. Without self-awareness, there is often a disconnect between your feelings and how you come across to people. You can unconsciously have an inability to see how you're impacting others with your words and actions. This is why Ralph had learned in his executive coaching sessions to be concerned about his impact on his colleagues, including the doctor. In cross-cultural conversations, your impact is as important as your intent.

CULTURAL INTELLIGENCE TOOL

Your impact is as important as your intent in cross-cultural conversations. After you make a statement, you can check your impact by asking:

- "What was the impact of my words?"
- "How did that land on you?"
- "What did you hear?"

Because you check the impact of your words and actions as a culturally intelligent leader, you'll notice that you're using your head, heart and hands to ultimately take action that's meaningful for all parties.

1. Head is thinking, acknowledging, seeing and understanding.

2. Heart is noticing and naming emotions, genuinely connecting with your own feelings and those of others in their circumstances and context.

3. Hands is demonstrating the compassion you feel through actions and behavioral change. It's adapting your behavior to show genuine respect for yourself and others, as well as setting compassionate boundaries for all involved. It's also about engaging the stakeholders and, together, implementing policies and practices in your community and organization that value people within their cultural context.

At the end of each of the following chapters, you'll have the opportunity to reflect on how you can use your head, heart and hands to extend your learning into a three-day challenge. You can record your learning, insights and questions from the three-day challenge in your journal. Also, because cultural intelligence is about developing the skills to talk with just about anyone, you may find it particularly helpful if you have a conversation partner with whom you can journey, laugh, love and learn.

CULTURAL INTELLIGENCE TOOL

To develop your cultural intelligence:

1. Select your journaling style. Dated events, reflections, insights and questions can be handwritten in a notebook, typed on a spreadsheet or spoken into an app. Take some time in the morning, midday or before bed to reflect and wonder. Record your insights and questions. If possible, take a moment, minute or hour to reflect on and care for you daily. After a few weeks of journaling, you may pick up on your own or other people's needs you hadn't seen before.

2. Find a Conversation Partner. This is a trusted friend, co-worker or colleague with whom you can share what's in your head and on your heart. You should feel safe with this person and make sure they care for you even when you feel you've messed up. Use this time to connect and experience compassion.

CHAPTER 2:
BUILDING COMMON VOCABULARY

If you talk to a man in a language he understands,
that goes to his head. If you talk to him in his language,
that goes to his heart.

-NELSON MANDELA

So much hinges on vocabulary, particularly when we're talking with someone who has a different background. If you don't have a shared understanding, you don't really know what a person means by a particular symbol, gesture, word or phrase. A shared understanding of symbols, gestures, words and phrases improves communication and builds trust. An example of how a word can mean different things in different contexts is if you ask someone from Alabama for a biscuit, you're likely to receive a hot, buttery, flaky, round, bread-based break-fast item. In London, if you ask for a biscuit, you're likely to get a room temperature, maybe buttery, crunchy, sweet cookie.

CASE STUDY:
JEFF'S STORY

An example of a symbol that can mean different things in different contexts is Jeff's flag. During a workshop I was facilitating at a corporation, Jeff, a mid-level retail manager, called me over to his group to ask a question. He wanted to know if he should have taken down his Confederate flag. I asked him where it was. He said, "It's on the wall of the garage." So I asked him what the problem was. He told me that it took up the better part of the back wall, and when the garage door was up, the neighbors could see it. I said, "I'm curious, what prompted you to put it up?"

Jeff said, "It represents part of U.S. history, my own history."

I said, "So it must be pretty important to you. Why did you think it needed to come down?"

Jeff explained, "After the Workshop last week, I got to thinking about what you'd said, that 'our impact is as important as our intent in cross-cultural conversations.' Because my neighbor is Black, I didn't want to hurt his feelings. So I took it down. Now I don't know if I did the right thing."

I said, "You've taken a great first step in building a relationship with your neighbor. You're thinking about how your actions impact him. That comes across as compassion."

Jeff said, "But I'm not sure if it helped to take it down."

I said, "Did you ask him?"

He said, "I wouldn't know what to say."

"What about saying what you just said to me? 'I took down the Confederate flag in my garage because I thought it might hurt your feelings. What was the impact of that flag on you?'"

Jeff said, "I can say that?"

I said, "Sure."

Jeff nodded and turned back to his group.

What happened

At the next workshop, I asked Jeff how it went. He said, "I didn't ask him because I decided the flag wasn't as important as our relationship."

I asked, "What did you do with your flag?"

Jeff said, "I didn't get rid of it; it's still important to me. I just found a more tactful place to put it up so I could honor our family history and take care of my neighbor, too. The best part is our families have been getting together every Sunday for barbecue dinners and really enjoy getting to know one another."

Later in the morning, Jeff pulled me aside and told me how grateful he was that he could be aware of his impact on other people. He said, "Checking my impact has led to this whole new friendship for us." Then he added, smiling, "It even helps with my wife!"

This ability to accept another person's perspective and adapt your words and actions to show genuine respect is cultural intelligence in action. That act of validating another person's feelings and experiences, even if you don't agree, is what creates a sense of belonging in any organization and community.

What are the 5 C's™ of Jeff's Story?

You can use the 5 C's™ as a tool to recognize how you're practicing cultural intelligence. Take a moment to consider how these five elements were apparent in Jeff's words and actions:

- Curiosity
- Contemplation
- Courage
- Context
- Compassion

When Jeff learned that symbols, gestures, words and phrases can impact different people differently, he got curious. He slowed down, was contemplative and considered the impact of his actions. He was courageous and asked for help. Our conversation allowed him the time to reflect on what the flag meant to him and could potentially mean for his neighbor. He demonstrated compassion for both himself and his neighbor by moving the flag to a place that allowed all parties to feel valued, heard, seen and engaged.

Culture

Our symbols, language and culture are inextricably linked. Language is the way people communicate with one another and construct culture. **Culture** is a set of beliefs, behaviors, values, assumptions, traditions and material objects that people in a particular group have in common. It is something that every group of two or more people — family, school, business, community center and country — shares.

From the story, Jeff and his neighbor are both Americans, husbands, sons, fathers and professionals who live in the same neighborhood. They have a lot in common. It's also apparent from the story that they have distinct family histories, language and skin colors. Their cultural commonalities and differences are manifest in both their visible and invisible cultures.

Visible culture refers to the easily observable and tangible aspects of a culture, like clothing, food, art, language, and rituals, that are readily apparent to people observing from the outside. Like Italian pizza, Chinese New Year or Mexican mariachi music. Humans recognize and appreciate cultural features they can see.

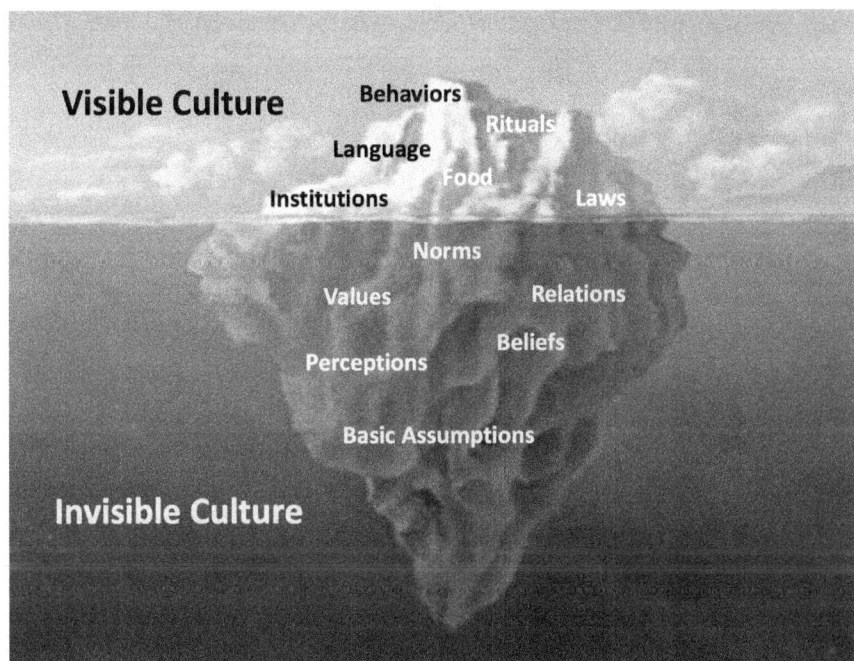

Visible Culture — Behaviors, Rituals, Language, Food, Institutions, Laws

Norms, Values, Relations, Perceptions, Beliefs, Basic Assumptions

Invisible Culture

The Cushner's Iceberg Model of Culture

Invisible culture is trickier because it is less tangible. **Invisible culture** is created by a group of people in the form of values, beliefs and perceptions that often guide a person but are not immediately apparent or tangible. People learn their values and beliefs from their families, places of worship, the media, school and work. Invisible culture is not necessarily appreciated by humans because it's hard to see.

When culture is unseen, unexamined or unchallenged, it's easy to think that your way of valuing, believing and perceiving is "normal." Being normal, you unconsciously express or act on your values. You don't think about your beliefs; you just believe them. This leaves you unaware of your impact. Initially, this was the case for Jeff. He had been raised with the confederate flag and was proud of his family's history. He's not wrong within his context. And he had not yet examined the meaning and impact of his flag from other cultural perspectives. However, when he came into contact with a different set of values, beliefs and perceptions, he became aware of the difference and its potential impact. The best part is he slowed down, got curious and asked for help to better understand.

When you don't know how to be curious about different values, beliefs and perceptions, you may feel challenged, awkward or threatened by that difference. You may think "this person or those people" are wrong. When you haven't thought much about or been exposed to cultural differences, defensive, awkward or angry feelings are a common human reaction. But this is why you're reading this book — to recognize your normal human feelings can be a stepping stone to learn more about yourself, your culture and other cultures. By reading this book, you're already developing your cultural self-awareness.

This cultural self-awareness you're developing is what allows you to confidently create a cohesive culture in your organization and community one conversation at a time.

> **PRO TIP:** It is helpful to know that when there is conflict or misunderstanding, it's typically because of differing and unexplored cultural characteristics that are invisible. Cultural self-awareness brings them into the light. In chapter 5, you'll learn more about specific cultural characteristics that influence how you think, feel, talk and act.

Two Elements of Every Culture

As you develop your cultural self-awareness, it's important to know there are two elements every culture has in common. Worldwide, within every country, community and organization of people, there are dominant and non-dominant cultural groups.

A dominant culture is one that is the most powerful, widespread or influential within a society or community where multiple cultures are present. In a society, it refers to the established language, religion, values, rituals and social customs that make it widely considered "the norm." In the case of Jeff, he was a part of the dominant culture.

In contrast, a **non-dominant culture** is a distinct group of people – differentiated by race, religion, caste, gender, wealth, health, disability, appearance, orientation, etc. – that coexists with but is subordinate to the dominant culture. Although not always, it is often smaller in number and is distinct from the dominant culture because of both visible and invisible cultural differences. In the case of Jeff, his neighbor was a part of the non-dominant culture.

Diversity

Diversity is variety – the opposite of sameness or homogeneous. When people speak about workplace diversity, there are often common, reflexive thoughts about extremes like Black/White, young/old or women/men. Yet, diversity comes in many forms. For example, Jeff and his neighbor were both educated, professional men who have families and yet they have different skin colors, histories, language and worldviews. It's helpful to know that diversity, like culture, can be seen and unseen. **Visible diversity** is age, gender, race, accent, physical disability and nationality. **Invisible diversity is** religion, education level, geographic background, travel experience, military background, neurodivergence, socio-economic status, etc.

Organizations benefit from recognizing that diverse backgrounds, different experiences and unique stories are important to their employees. When employees feel valued, heard, seen and engaged for their uniqueness, the organization and the community experience more engagement, commitment and collaboration.

PRO TIP: So often, when an organization initially seeks to diversify, they look for people with visible differences. However, if the goal is greater engagement, collaboration and commitment, you need to be cognizant of and appreciate both visible and invisible differences.

Organizations and communities also benefit by recognizing how a person looks or identifies directly impacts their productivity and ability to reach their potential. It impacts their safety, health and emotional well-being and their ability to navigate educational, financial and legal systems.

One study found that employees of color not only encounter more negative incidents than their White counterparts at work, they also miss out on experiences that leave them feeling good. That gap in positive experiences accounts for a 10-15% difference in attrition for employees of color and Whites (Norlander, P., Does, S. & Shih, M., 2019). That means retention is not just about avoiding negative experiences for employees of color but also about having positive experiences. Examples of positive experiences include going out for coffee, career mapping, mentoring and receiving regular constructive feedback.

CULTURAL INTELLIGENCE TOOL

To learn how employees of color and those from historically marginalized groups are impacted by their visible and invisible differences in your workplace or community center, you can notice and address:

- Who is and is not talking in meetings?
- Who is not in the room that is impacted by decisions being made?
- Who is and is not in the organization that would increase innovation and market reach?
- Who in the meeting and organization is being overlooked, undervalued or discouraged?

Belonging

It's pretty easy to tell when you, your ideas or your effort aren't appreciated or accepted. Feeling sidelined or silenced hurts and drives people out of the organization. On the other hand, employees don't just want to be included, they want to be integral to the team. They want to belong. So, what is belonging?

Belonging in a group is a feeling of acceptance, whereby each group member feels valued, heard, seen and engaged by other group members and is able to reciprocate and provide that experience for fellow group members as well. Culturally intelligent organizations are intentional about building a culture of appreciation, belonging and connection.

Belonging occurs in an organization when:

- People feel valued, heard, seen and engaged, by everyone and particularly by the dominant group members.
- People and their experiences are vital to the group and bring vitality to the group.
- Dominant and non-dominant group member voices count, have influence and are seen as assets.
- Leaders acknowledge and support cultural differences.
- Cultural differences are seen as an asset to the organization and market.

When everyone experiences this sense of belonging, there's more genuine care, collaboration, commitment and retention in any organization and community.

CASE STUDY:
BELONGING

Andrea, a marketing specialist, and Evan, a software engineer, started work on the same Monday at a tech startup company. Each attended orientation sessions for the company and their respective departments. By Friday, Andrea's head was swimming in a sea of acronyms used in the company that made her feel like she was drowning in alphabet soup. She was unsure if the acronyms were company-related or tech-related and was afraid asking would make her look underqualified for her job.

At lunch, Evan saw Andrea sitting alone, looking a little exhausted. He asked to join her. As he sat down, he said, "I'm going to have to create a chart to remember all the acronyms used around here!" Andrea perked up and laughed in agreement. Together they made a list of the ones they could remember. That weekend Evan put their list on a shared cloud document so he and Andrea could continue adding new acronyms they learned.

A few months later, Evan found himself on a company holiday party committee creating an acronym bingo game from his and Andrea's acronym list. It was a big hit at the party. When the CEO asked Evan where the idea came from, he pulled Andrea into the conversation and shared the story of his and Andrea's bonding over their early acronym overwhelm. The CEO was surprised and saw an opportunity, "Would the two of you assist the hiring committee on a short project by helping them incorporate your acronym list and game into the new hire materials? This is really great information. Thank you."

When you see and feel a connection with others, you realize that all people struggle and have difficult times. You realize you're not alone; there is comfort in that knowledge – like Andrea, Evan and the acronym alphabet soup. To accept others and their differing perspectives often requires that you slow down and take the time to be open to finding value in the other person's ideas or thought process. Even when you don't agree with that person, if you stay open, you can discover a place of connection, a common interest or a shared point of pain. Over time that connection helps to grow a sense of belonging.

CULTURAL INTELLIGENCE TOOL

In the place of correction, create connection to communicate acceptance and a sense of belonging.

What are the 5 C's™ of Andrea and Evan's story?

Take a few minutes to consider how the 5 Cs apply in the case study about Andrea and Evan:

- Curiosity
- Contemplation
- Courage
- Context
- Compassion

BREATHE AND RELAX

Contemplation takes practice. It can be challenging if it's new. Even within the process of learning how to contemplate, it's important to care for yourself. Work gently toward a daily practice, even if it's just a moment or minute. Take the time to do a few deep belly breaths. Then put your hands over your heart space. Hold your heart as you would a puppy – with tenderness. Lower your gaze to your heart. Any thoughts that come up, send them down to your heart and offer them some grace. This allows you to be gentler and kinder with yourself as you learn and grow your cultural intelligence. An added benefit is that as you come to feel for yourself, you can more genuinely feel with and care for others.

CONVERSATION PARTNER

Because cultural intelligence is about building relationships across cultural groups and valuing both similarities and differences so that they feel valued, heard, seen and engaged, it's important to reflect on and share your learning with a Conversation Partner.

Consider sharing what you wrote in your journal with your partner and listen as they share what they learned. Discussing your individual insights may surface new learnings that weren't in your journal.

THREE-DAY CHALLENGE

Because your impact is as important as your intent in cross-cultural conversations, language matters. What you say and how you say it can make the difference between a person staying or leaving your organization or community. To genuinely connect with another person and create a cohesive culture, use your head, heart and hands to notice, feel and act with cultural intelligence.

During the next three days, observe, experience and practice with language.

Day 1: Today, listen for the words people use in different contexts. Use your head, heart and hands to reflect on and write in your journal:

1. What words do people of dominant and non-dominant cultural groups use?
2. What words do people use to either minimize or appreciate people and their unique backgrounds?
3. What words do you inadvertently or intentionally use to create a connection with another person?

Day 2: Today, notice and name the impact of language on you and others.

1. List the times you wish people were more aware of the impact of their words.
2. What words make you and/or others feel dismissed, sidelined or silenced?
3. What do you wish could be done differently to help you and others feel a sense of belonging?

Day 3: Today, watch how language impacts groups of people in your organization or community.

1. What language practice inadvertently or intentionally leaves people feeling sidelined or silenced?
2. How is that impact on people made apparent?
3. What cultural intelligence tools can you use to take a first step so that people feel more valued, heard, seen and engaged?

CHAPTER 3:
MAKING THE CASE
FOR DIVERSITY

Intelligence is the ability to adapt to change.

- STEPHEN HAWKING

Diversity is a buzzword. Some people are sick of it and think or say, "We've got it already. Look at all the progress we've made." Others say, "We haven't done enough. Equity in our institutions hasn't been achieved. With all the talk about diversity, is it worth the effort?"

I began to wonder what the research had to say. I wanted to know if diversifying an organization was worth the effort. Amid economic uncertainty, finding and retaining employees is important. And because generations Y and Z are so demographically diverse and each generation coming up is even more diverse, we won't be able to hire only people who look and act like us. This isn't all bad because a global consulting firm found that companies with the most ethnic diversity on their executive team are 43% more likely to experience higher profitability (McKinsey & Co., 2018).

But, because I know there is potential for conflict and hurt when diverse opinions are present, I wanted to learn more. I found other research that said merely making an organization look more diverse but not training leaders and employees to appreciate differences actually lowers performance because it increases stereotyping and stonewalling (Maznevski & DiStefano, 2012).

So wouldn't it just be easier to keep an organization homogenous? Based on that same body of research, the answer is no. The research shows that when leaders and employees are trained to appreciate and talk about differences, multicultural teams significantly outperform mono-cultural teams. When leaders and employees have the skills to ensure their colleagues feel valued, heard, seen and engaged, that's what increases retention, engagement, collaboration and profitability. That's when diversity actually works in favor of the organization.

Cultural Intelligence is CRITICAL to Team Performance

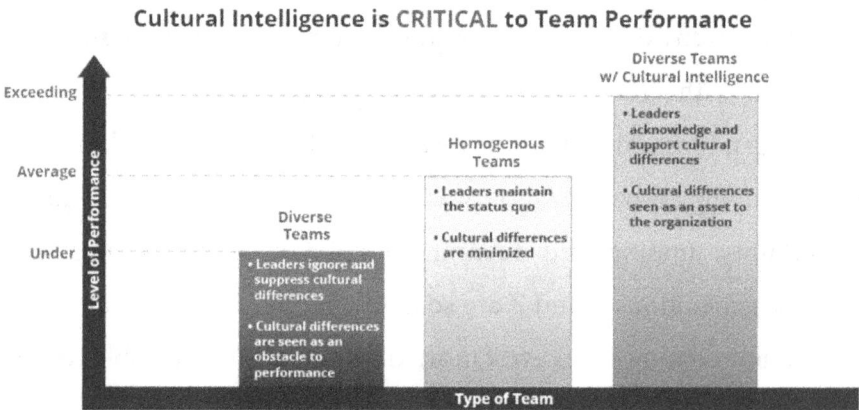

Reference: Distefano, J.J, Maznevski M Creating Value with Diverse Teams in Global Management, Organisational Dynamics, Vol 29, No 1, pp 45-53, 2000

This research also suggests that people from non-dominant cultural groups may not be reflected in innovation-contribution and decision-making positions in organizations. Yet, their presence on a team, along with the ability to successfully navigate cross-cultural conversations, invigorates innovation, mitigates risk with diverse markets and creates potential for higher profitability than do homogeneous teams. This is what Bob and Dan discovered by using their cultural intelligence to talk and work successfully with people of different backgrounds and skills.

CASE STUDY:

THE VALUE OF DIVERSITY

Dan and Bob talked monthly at their local coffee roaster's association meeting, sharing friendship and knowledge. While there was a difference in age and style, and sometimes head-to-head competition, both leaders respected and admired each other. Dan, an entrepreneur in his 30s, launched his company only eight years ago. While Bob, a 40-year veteran of the business world and in his 60s, is the fourth generation to own the family business.

When Bob first met Dan in the 1990s, he did not think the starry-eyed young man asking him to join a coffee association had a chance to bring together a group of established companies like his with all his hipster ideas. Heck, Bob's company received their first coffee beans from South America via steamboat 100 years ago! What could they possibly need to learn about the coffee business?!

Over time, though, Bob's company learned a lot from the coffee hipster, not about roasting, but about people. Until Dan talked about how the diversity of his employees helped him innovate, learn, understand and reach new markets, Bob's company had never even considered anything other than premium coffee sold to the finest restaurants, hotels and high-end grocery stores across the United States. His experience was with other college-educated, wealthy, white Americans who networked and sold to other businesses owned primarily by people who identified with similar backgrounds.

Although he had never thought about it before, Bob realized his bias was with his family's values system – that coffee suggested elegance and sophistication, priced for the wealthy.

Dan, also white, was born in the same town as Bob. However, Dan had been raised in Ethiopia with a family in the diplomatic core. The family home was surrounded by coffee farms. Dan not only knew the roasting and the importing side of the business, he knew the years of cultivating it took to grow excellent beans enjoyed by laborers and farmers as well as presidents and monarchs around the world. He saw coffee as art created by people for all types of people to enjoy.

Dan found baristas to design and serve coffee as art. He encouraged the coffee roaster's association to hold bean roasting and tasting competitions to celebrate the best in the industry, from the bush to the cup. He hired experienced professionals from every corner of the world and people from completely different backgrounds whose only outstanding quality was a passion for coffee. He listened, smiled, learned and talked with everyone.

After taking a tour of the startup, Bob asked Dan, "How do you keep everyone working so well together?" Bob's all-male, mostly white (except for a few dock workers) staff ran like clockwork, reproducing daily what had been done for a century – but was very plain-vanilla compared to Dan's employees. Dan replied, "I don't. They do! There's an African proverb I always thought rang true, 'When you want to go fast, go alone. If you want to go far, go together.'"

"I don't get it," Bob said. "How does that translate into business practices for you?"

"When we hire, we look for experience for some roles, but in all roles, we look for unique perspectives, personalities and passions that truly believe the next best innovation or process could come from anyone, even themselves. From there, we keep shaping an environment of active listening, experimenting, collaborating and applauding mistakes as a step on the road to success. We also built a system to document our successes so we know how to replicate them and document our mistakes so we only make them once," shared Dan.

This was the conversation that prompted Bob to start envisioning how he might begin to guide his company to innovate and grow for the next 100 years. He would consider the diverse marketplace and employee base more than his great-grandfather had ever envisioned when he founded the company. Bob first began to welcome ideas, mistakes and successes from everyone. Then, he hired people with different perspectives and backgrounds than his own. Today, with Robert Jr. as chairman of the board, the company profitably sells coffee worldwide, and their annual staff picture looks like a photo from the United Nations.

What are the 5 C's™ of Bob and Dan's story?

Take a few minutes to consider how the 5 Cs apply in the case study about Bob and Dan:

- Curiosity
- Contemplation
- Courage
- Context
- Compassion

Culturally intelligent leaders like Bob acknowledge and support cultural differences and recognize them as vital assets to the organization. With cultural intelligence, organizations like Bob's experience:

- Improved employee engagement for everyone in the organization.
- The ability to hire, retain and promote diverse talent without alienating anyone.
- A culture of belonging and safety resulting in increased productivity and commitment.
- An ever-broader market share and client diversity.
- International business adaptation and job performance.
- International transfer of technology and job performance.
- Revenue growth because employees and customers feel confident about working with just about anyone.

FIVE STAGES OF CULTURAL INTELLIGENCE

As is apparent in the case of Bob, cultural intelligence isn't something you just have; rather, cultural intelligence is grown and developed. There are five stages of development: Denial, Polarization, Minimization, Acceptance and Adaptation. To learn your ability level to navigate conversations with people who are different, you and/or your team can take the Intercultural Development Inventory® (IDI®) developed by Dr. Mitch Hammer. The IDI is a 50-item online inventory that assesses an individual's and group's ability to navigate cross-cultural conversations effectively. The IDI has been used by over 4,000 organizations and educational institutions worldwide and taken by over one million people globally. According to Hammer (2011) the average distribution of the mindsets is roughly:

3% – Denial

15% – Polarization

65% – Minimization

15% – Acceptance

2% – Adaptation

CULTURAL INTELLIGENCE TOOL

To uncover your team's current mindset, reach out to take the Intercultural Development Inventory® (IDI®)
Email: Info@EmpoweringPartners.com.

Intercultural Development Continuum (IDC)©

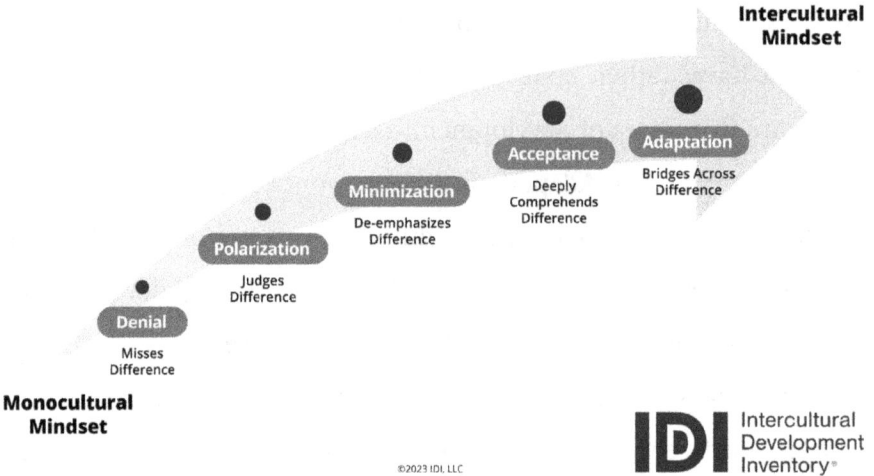

Intercultural Mindset

Adaptation
Bridges Across Difference

Acceptance
Deeply Comprehends Difference

Minimization
De-emphasizes Difference

Polarization
Judges Difference

Denial
Misses Difference

Monocultural Mindset

©2023 IDI, LLC

IDI Intercultural Development Inventory®

Knowing the five stages, or mindsets, of cultural intelligence and their definitions helps you and your team envision and navigate next steps so that people in your organization and community feel valued, heard, seen and engaged.

- **Denial** is little to no recognition of more complex cultural differences. It is often unintended and due to missing cultural differences of people.
- **Polarization** is a judgmental orientation toward cultural commonalities and differences; it has a binary mindset – "us versus them."
- **Minimization** highlights cultural commonalities that can mask deeper recognition of cultural differences; it believes a focus on commonalities is best.

- **Acceptance** is being curious about and interested in cultural commonalities and differences in their own and other cultures; it sees diversity as an asset but is unclear how to adapt behavior to show genuine respect.

- **Adaptation** is the ability to appreciate another cultural perspective and shift words and actions to show genuine respect within the cultural context. People who reach this stage recognize their own cultural systems of power and influence and choose to use their power to ensure each voice feels valued and engaged.

From the mindset of **Adaptation**, a person embraces an **intercultural mindset** that supports, advocates and allows for the expression of multiple cultural group perspectives. However, in most workplaces and communities, **Minimization** is the dominant cultural mindset. In this case, **cultural assimilation** takes the form of "sink or swim" for new hires. Within this **monocultural mindset**, leaders typically assume new hires can figure out how things are done in an organization, "just like I did." This can have negative consequences; individuals with diverse backgrounds can be left feeling ignored and sidelined because their contributions go unrecognized.

- **Cultural assimilation** is when a person or group absorbs, resembles or assumes the values, behaviors and beliefs of the dominant group, whether fully or partially. This is done inadvertently or intentionally.

- **Monocultural mindset** is a mindset that supports, advocates or allows for the expression of a single cultural group perspective.
- **Intercultural mindset** is a mindset that supports, advocates or allows for the expression of multiple cultural group perspectives.

PRO TIP: What often surprises people is that two-thirds of the population worldwide are unknowingly stuck in the mindset of Minimization. Because of this, there is often strong pressure for people of all backgrounds to conform to the dominant culture and maintain its status quo.

To upend Minimization and its impact, and move toward an **intercultural mindset,** you'll need to develop cultural self-awareness *and* other-awareness. You can do this by becoming aware of your reactions, assumptions, values, word choices, and their impact on others. With self-awareness, you naturally and intentionally begin to slow down and shift from reacting to others to responding with a cool head. This was the case for Macy.

CASE STUDY:
HOW TO DEVELOP CULTURAL INTELLIGENCE

Macy, a 45-year-old executive at a Fortune 500 company, is a well-traveled professional who enjoys using her cultural intelligence to stay in touch with her emotions and genuinely connect with colleagues and clients.

Because she's culturally self-aware, she noticed that each time she met with an Arab or German member of her company or client's company, she felt a knot in her stomach and a rising sense of distrust. As Macy learned more about the other person though, their business needs, values and context, her sense of distrust would dissipate.

Alone, Macy began to reflect on and wonder about these feelings of distrust. She noticed that her initial feelings were often draining, distracting and difficult. As her cultural intelligence training had taught her, she started to notice and name her assumptions and feelings when they came up, became curious about them and made notes in her journal.

With her journal in hand one morning, she sat quietly and contemplated her notes. She began to remember many happy times with her grandmother. As a young girl, Macy spent many Friday afternoons in her grandmother's kitchen learning to make traditional dishes for that evening's dinner. Macy thought it was odd that this memory surfaced first, but then she remembered: The cooking lessons often came with life lessons from her grandmother.

As a young girl, Macy's grandmother fled Germany with her family and settled in Israel. Her grandmother's Jewish family had learned to be very fearful of both Germans and Arabs from their experience. Once Macy identified the feelings and the root cause, she stayed with them and came to feel a sense of compassion for herself. Now, when Macy meets people who are Arabic and German, she feels and acknowledges a pang of sadness for her grandmother's experience. At the same time, she feels a sense of curiosity and even some joy about getting to know new people. With new-found self-awareness and tenderness, she realizes that her fears are real and also that they belonged to her grandmother within her specific place and time. Now, Macy feels grateful for the ability that cultural intelligence has given her – to experience each individual with wonder, perspective and connection.

In the Appendix under, *Self-Awareness is Key to a Cohesive Culture*, you can read more about how to develop self-awareness and manage your thoughts, feelings and actions.

What are the 5 C's™ of Macy's story?

Take a few minutes to consider how the 5 C's™ apply in the case study about Macy:

- Curiosity
- Contemplation
- Courage
- Context
- Compassion

SLOW DOWN

Macy slowed down and got contemplative. She acknowledged her difficult feelings. She became aware of the contrast between her own curiosity and the natural suspicion of her grandmother based on their unique contexts. Had she not taken that time to acknowledge and accept those differences in their experiences, Macy would have inadvertently been practicing Minimization. Had she not developed this cultural self-awareness and overcome the Minimization, she would not have been aware of her antagonism and the resulting subtle impact of her words and actions on her German and Arabic colleagues and clients.

Minimizing or ignoring "different-ness" creates an environment in which people tend to focus on what everybody has in common and assume that others with the same experiences or opportunities are the same. Focusing on what we all have in common may be well intended in a dominant culture, but the impact is dismissive of your own and others' humanity.

CULTURAL INTELLIGENCE TOOL

So that you don't inadvertently sideline or silence a colleague, client, friend or family member, it's helpful to be aware of what Minimization can sound like. Depending on the context, a minimizing remark or question can be:

- "Just get over it."
- "I don't see color."
- "That's not sexist, is it?"
- "This too shall pass."
- "As long as they can do the job, does it matter where they're from?"
- "Oh, you're fine."
- "I don't know what your problem is."
- "At least you still have a job."

When you or someone makes a remark that is inadvertently or intentionally belittling to you or another, it can be off-putting, harmful and destructive to an individual and the entire culture of an organization or community.

When a destructive remark is made, how do you respond if you need to stay in relationship with that colleague, client, community member, friend or family member?

CULTURAL INTELLIGENCE TOOL

S.T.O.P. is an acronym for one of your most powerful tools for creating genuine connections within yourself and with others:

- **S** – Slow Down.
- **T** – Take three deep breaths.
- **O** – Observe your feelings, notice your assumption and how the other person might be feeling.
  If you are physically and psychologically safe,
- **P** – Proceed with a softer gaze of curiosity and wonder.

You **S.T.O.P.** – Slow down, Take three deep breaths, Observe your feelings, notice your assumption and how the other person might be feeling, and, if you're safe, Proceed with curiosity and wonder into the conversation. Before you say or do anything, the goal is to get contemplative – take a moment, minute, hour or day, whatever time it takes to care for you – and shift from a mindless reaction to a thoughtful response.

This doesn't mean you ignore or deny your anger; that would be minimization in play. On the contrary, by applying S.T.O.P., you acknowledge your anger and give yourself the grace, space and time you need to recover and get more information so that your perspective softens a bit. That moment, minute, hour or day that you take is your gift to yourself and it's where your power lies. S.T.O.P. is one of your most powerful tools for cultural intelligence that can save your relationship, job and/or career.

CULTURAL INTELLIGENCE TOOL

If you're physically and psychologically safe, to proceed with curiosity and wonder so that you can appreciate their experience, you might ask:

- Do you mind if I ask you a question?
- What has been your experience?
- How did you feel about that?
- What was the impact of my words?

CASE STUDY:
APPLY S.T.O.P.

Jason, a White man, was really angry about being laid off. During the morning coffee break, he made a racist remark about Black workers and their lack of qualifications. Rather than ignore the statement, which is Minimization in action, Mandy wanted to use her cultural intelligence. First, she used S.T.O.P – Slow down, take a breath and observe and feel her upset.

Next, she proceeded with curiosity and wonder by using questions like the ones listed above. She wanted to slow the conversation down to learn more about Jason's experience. With these steps, cultural intelligence helped Mandy safely learn what prompted Jason to make the remark. While she didn't agree with his words, she was able to appreciate his experience and feelings. This allowed Jason to feel the compassion he needed to feel seen and heard.

This, in turn, allowed Mandy to address her concern at a time when Jason is acting more like himself. So often, when a person feels seen and heard, it's then that they're able to offer grace in return. This is how the conversation unfolded:

Mandy: "Do you mind if I ask you a question?"

Jason: "Sure."

Mandy: "What happened that made you so angry?"

Jason: "The company needed to increase their affirmative action numbers; I have the least seniority here, so they're letting me go at the end of this month."

Mandy: "Ouch! That's gotta be tough!"

Jason: "You're not kidding. I have no idea how I am going to pay the bills while I look for another job."

Mandy: "That sounds scary. Let me know if you want to put our heads together and brainstorm."

Jason: "I appreciate your understanding. I'll let you know."

While the racist remark offended Mandy, she recognized Jason's words were coming from a place of fear and pain. When she slowed down, she realized at that moment that he needed someone to show compassion and feel with him. This was not the time to correct him; it was the time to connect with him. At a later date, when Jason is acting more like himself, Mandy will be able to circle back and share with him how his remark impacted her.

What are the 5 C's™ of Mandy and Jason's story?

Take a few minutes to consider how the 5 C's™ apply in the case study about Mandy and Jason:

- Curiosity
- Contemplation
- Courage
- Context
- Compassion

CULTURAL INTELLIGENCE TOOL

Here are five ways to slow down a conversation so that you both can take a breath and get more perspective:

1. "I need a minute to think this through."

2. "Help me understand your perspective."

3. "That's interesting – can you tell me more?"

4. "Let me reflect on this and I'll circle back with you."

5. "This is good input. Let's explore this along with other options and see what we like best."

BREATHE AND RELAX

As you've gained new experiences and insight in this chapter, take a contemplative moment or minute to breathe, relax and recognize yourself for showing up for this work. A way to breathe and relax is by feeling your feet. Sit up straight in your chair, put your feet flat on the floor and intentionally focus on the sensation of your feet making contact with the ground. This simple technique is used to bring your awareness to the present moment and create a sense of stability by connecting with your physical body. Essentially, it's a way to anchor yourself to the "here and now" by paying attention to the physical sensations under your feet.

THREE-DAY CHALLENGE

During the next three days, observe, experience and upend the impact of Minimization. Use your head, heart and hands to reflect on and write in your journal:

Day 1: Today, look for examples of words and actions that minimize people.

1. What is said and done to minimize?
2. Under what circumstances do you minimize yourself and other people?
3. Who in your organization or community gets minimized?

Day 2: Today, observe your feelings and the reactions of others when minimization happens.

1. How do you feel when you or what you do gets minimized?
2. How do others react when they or their work gets minimized?
3. How did your observations make you look at yourself and other people differently?

Day 3: Today, watch for the impact of minimization and the potential for acceptance.

1. What words and actions can you use to accept yourself as you are, even when you make a mistake or have a lesson to learn?

2. What practice or policy in your organization or community inadvertently or intentionally leaves people feeling minimized?

3. What cultural intelligence tool can you use to take a first step so that more people feel accepted, or in other words, valued, heard, seen and engaged?

CHAPTER 4:
OUTSMARTING ASSUMPTIONS

We can be blind to the obvious,
and we are also blind to our blindness.

- DANIEL KAHNEMAN

When talking with another person, if you don't slow down and recognize the assumptions you hold about them or their situation, you run the risk of missing the opportunity for genuine connection and real problem solving. When the conversation shuts down, you both can end up feeling alienated and you risk losing that employee, community member or stakeholder. That was the case for the CEO, Chuck.

In an executive coaching session, Chuck had a question for me. He wanted to know what to do about an employee who was always late. I said, "Are you asking me because the employee is Black?"

He looked at me kind of sheepishly and said, "If my White employees are consistently late, they have already been fired. I don't know what to do about this guy. Should I call my Black pastor friend and see if he'll have a talk with him?"

I said, "That's a good question. I appreciate that you're working to figure out the best way to communicate effectively with your employee. Can I ask you a question? [Chuck nodded.] Is it a sustainable solution to call your Black pastor friend each time there's an issue with a Black employee? Perhaps it would be more effective to empower the manager."

Chuck said, "Yeah, you're right. His manager should learn how to deal with these issues. We all obviously have something to learn here."

I said, "The first question is, do you want to keep this employee? Is he worth pursuing?"

Chuck told me the employee is a good worker once he's on-site. He said, "Besides, I didn't grow up in this country, so I know the value of having different perspectives in the plant. So, what do we need to do?"

I said, "Since you don't want to lose him, his manager needs to have a conversation with the employee. Sounds like you may have made an assumption about him because he's Black. Assumptions are bits of knowledge about a person or group that we humans accept as true, but without proof – of which we are many times unaware. We're unaware of the assumptions because they're encountered so often in our cultural environment that we think they are normal. It's not your fault per se. But now that you know better, you and your manager can do better by your employee and get the rest of his story.

Chuck nodded and agreed to get more of the story.

What happened?

Later on that week, I followed up with Chuck. He said he and the plant manager had a conversation with the employee. They recognized their assumptions had been getting in the way of really listening to the employee's story.

They learned that the employee was often late because the public transportation wasn't reliable. He didn't have a car and, because the factory is in a remote part of town, it's hard to get to work. And even if he did have a car, he had recently lost his license.

The plant manager helped him find an apartment within walking distance of the factory and fronted him the money for the first month's rent and security deposit. The employee has since paid back the loan and is consistently on time for work.

Like Chuck discovered, in this chapter, you'll learn how to be on the lookout for assumption(s) that may get in the way of learning a person's story. When you take the time to learn their story, you can often uncover the root cause and create a genuine connection. That's what creates better working conditions and a more cohesive culture for everyone.

What are the 5 C's™ of Chuck's story?

Take a few minutes to consider how the 5 C's™ apply in the case study about Chuck:

- Curiosity
- Contemplation
- Courage

- Context
- Compassion

Chuck and his plant manager were able to come to a shared understanding with their employee. Chuck applied the cultural intelligence tool, S.T.O.P. By slowing down, taking a deep breath and observing his assumption, he learned more about the employee's situation. With a shared understanding, the employee got a home that was more conveniently located, and Chuck retained a trained, hard-working employee. This ability to create a win-win scenario for all parties is cultural intelligence in action.

UNCONSCIOUS BIAS

Initially, Chuck didn't realize he had a hidden assumption about his employee, that is until he asked for help. Hidden assumptions are bits of knowledge about a person or group that you accept as true – without proof – of which you are unaware. These assumptions are stored in our brains and encountered so often in our cultural environment that we think they are normal. And because we view them as normal, we're unaware that they influence how we think, speak and act. This is also called **unconscious bias** (Banaji and Greenwald, 2013).

It can be hard to imagine you have mental content in your brains that you're unconscious of. Here's an example of how you can be tricked into thinking you know when you don't actually know. Consider this:

What is the relationship between squares A and B in the images?

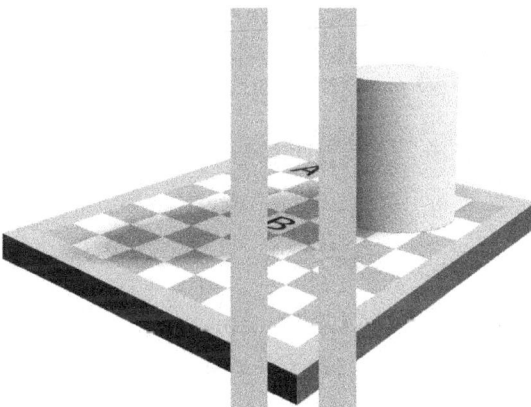

It's hard to believe squares A and B are the same shade of gray. Even when you put the squares side-by-side, and you can see they are the same shade, your brain can be convinced the squares are different. To see the truth about the shades of gray, you really have to slow down your thinking and get more information.

THINK, FAST AND SLOW

Daniel Kahneman, author of *Thinking, Fast and Slow* (2011), explains there are two different ways the brain forms thoughts: fast and slow. Thinking fast is effortless and quick. Humans spend most of their time thinking fast. It's easier, after all.

Thinking fast is a characteristic of unconscious bias. Biased thinking isn't bad or good. It's normal. It helps you think quickly and efficiently. Within milliseconds, it helps you assess if a person, group or situation is a friend or foe. Every human being does this. Because you, like all other humans, have a fundamental need to feel safe, you cannot help categorizing people, groups and situations by their differences.

Biased thinking is normal to you and me because of how we've been shaped by the culture around us since the beginning of time - through repeated exposure to images in movies, news, jokes and stories we've learned from family, school, work, places of worship and community. It's nothing to be ashamed of; it's part of being human.

Interestingly enough, though, biased thinking is accurate 70% of the time. That fact, along with the fact that biased thinking keeps us humans safe, made me wonder, what's the problem with it? The problem is that even with it being accurate 70% of the time, the information you have is limited. It's not the whole story.

That was the case for Chuck and his employee. Thinking fast, he thought he knew something about his employee. But when Chuck learned how bias works in his brain, he realized he may need to get more of the story in order to retain his employee. In this process of getting more of the story, you can create a connection with employees and come to a shared understanding.

CULTURAL INTELLIGENCE TOOL

Observing your thinking is what empowers you to shift from reaction to response.

- **Unconscious bias** or hidden assumptions occur automatically when the brain makes fast judgments based on experiences and/or background. That fast thinking results in prejudice or unsupported judgments in favor of or against one thing, person or group as compared to another. With unconscious biases, certain people benefit, and other people do not.

- **Fast thinking** is instinctive, automatic, incomplete, effortless and biased and often includes flawed thought fragments. This is how brains prefer to function, held over from a time when fight or flight was necessary for survival.

- **Slow thinking** is slowing down, taking a breath, noticing your assumptions and proceeding with curiosity and wonder to get more information about a person or situation.

- **Stereotyping** is categorizing people, groups and situations based on fast thinking and oversimplification.

A shared understanding comes with thinking slow(ly), not fast. **Fast thinking** is instinctive, automatic, incomplete, effortless, stereotyping, biased and includes thought fragments. This is how brains prefer to function; it's a holdover from a time when fight/flight was necessary for survival.

Slow thinking is slowing down, taking a breath and noticing your assumptions long enough to hold them a little more lightly. With that extra moment or minute, the mental space can open up and your gaze softens. That's when you can proceed with curiosity and wonder to get more information about a person or situation. An everyday example of thinking fast is, "I need to go to the grocery store." Thinking slowly, though, you consider a way to ultimately save time and be more productive: "I need to make a grocery list."

CULTURAL INTELLIGENCE TOOL

In your workplace or community center, you may hear a culturally intelligent leader slow down and say:

- "More important than talking, I need to listen and learn."
- "We can be more constructive and build people up rather than tear people down."
- "It's comforting to know I'm not the only one seeing the problem; it's good to talk."
- "To get more information, I need to ask more questions rather than assume I know."
- "If this person is struggling, I wonder if there are others that are similarly impacted."
- "Is this behavior we're seeing a character defect or a cultural default?"
- "Are we minimizing the human element in our organization by always prioritizing accomplishments?"
- "To genuinely care for my team, I need to care for myself first."

CASE STUDY:
ASSUMPTIONS ABOUT LATIN CULTURES

Beth, a world-traveled, multiracial woman, met Javier at a networking event and was instantly dazzled by his work experience, easy smile and infectious humor. Because of all her Mexican, Costa Rican, Peruvian and Spanish friends, Beth felt comfortable talking with Latinos.

Javier's Venezuelan accent and sense of humor felt familiar to her. The next week, when Beth met Javier at her favorite Mexican restaurant to discuss a potential joint project between their companies, Beth was very surprised when Javier said, "What do you recommend? I don't know anything about Mexican food." She described several dishes to Javier. Once he had made a choice, she asked him if he would mind telling her about Venezuelan food and what is unique to his country. He was happy she'd asked. Not surprisingly, she learned that quesillo, similar to Mexico's flan, is a favorite traditional dessert. But she was surprised to learn that tortillas are not popular in Venezuela; arepas are the staple. Beth was equally surprised to learn that lasagna, which Beth thought was strictly Italian, is called pasticho in Venezuela, where it is a dish of great national pride. Beth and Javier went on to enjoy lunch and a successful business venture.

What are the 5 C's™ of Beth's story?

Take a few minutes to consider how the 5 C's™ apply in the case study about Beth.

- Curiosity
- Contemplation
- Courage
- Context
- Compassion

TYPES OF BIAS

With her vast experience, Beth could have assumed she knew all about the foods from Latin America. Instead, she slowed down, got contemplative and expressed her curiosity. It takes courage to adopt a posture of learning and growing. Learning more about the Venezuelan context, she felt compassion and experienced the fun, food and a new relationship.

Not all biased thinking and blind spots are labeled, but some are so common they are given names. The good news is that once named, they're easier to notice, name and ultimately debunk.

One example of an unconscious bias is called **confirmation bias**. In our earlier story, Chuck's actions were initially influenced by this common thinking mistake. Confirmation bias is the tendency to over-value data and observations that fit with or confirm our existing beliefs.

While it seems obvious enough to avoid, it's a particularly sinister kind of bias because it affects not just intellectual or political debates but also our relationships, personal finances, and even our physical and mental health. Here's how it can trick us into rejecting something unfamiliar.

When a brain comes across new information, people or situations, within nanoseconds, it makes snap decisions without our permission. The steps go something like this:

1. The brain checks: What do I already believe?
2. If a new idea fits, that's easy and efficient – the brain hits "Accept."
3. If a new idea doesn't fit, that's hard and inefficient – the brain hits "Reject," because hard work equals pain.

If it's hard and painful, the brain rejects the information, people or situation within nanoseconds. That's what can inadvertently block us from a connection and hurt a relationship.

CULTURAL INTELLIGENCE TOOL

Self-awareness is key to upending bias. Though there are hundreds of biases, here are seven common thinking mistakes:

- **Dunning-Kruger Effect bias** is cognitive bias, where a person with a low level of knowledge in a particular subject mistakenly assesses their knowledge or ability as greater than it is.

- **Negativity bias** is cognitive bias, where a person irrationally weighs the potential for a negative outcome as more important than that of the positive outcome.

- **Self-Serving Effect bias** is cognitive bias where a person inaccurately attributes successes to themselves and failure to interference by other people or situations.

- **The Curse of Knowledge and Hindsight biases** are cognitive biases where a person assumes others know the same information and/or have the same experiences.

- **Optimism/Pessimism biases** are cognitive biases where a person's mood or outlook inaccurately shapes their belief. If we feel good, our bias is to a positive outcome, and when we feel bad, our bias is to a negative outcome.

- **Backfire Effect bias** is cognitive bias where a person reactively clings harder or defends a belief with more force after it has been challenged.

- **In-Group bias** is cognitive bias where a person unfairly favors or prefers someone in their own group or someone like them over other people.

CULTURAL INTELLIGENCE TOOL

Find a person at a social event with whom you might not normally speak. Use these steps to practice creating a connection and relating to that person:

1. Feel the tendency to move away from someone who seems different.

2. Notice an assumption that comes up and hold it lightly until you get more information.

3. Ensure that you're physically and emotionally safe.

4. Ask an open-ended question to take an interest in the person.

Go-slow conversation starters:

- What's your passion?

- What's your favorite family tradition?

- When you're on a business trip, what do you like to do with your downtime?

- What has been your experience living/working here?

HOW TO SEEK A SHARED UNDERSTANDING

To avoid hurting a relationship and/or alienating a colleague, client, family member, friend or community member, you can work toward a shared understanding like Chuck did. The graphic below illustrates how to seek shared understanding with another person.

To reach a shared understanding, this is the path:

1. You see and hear another's words and actions.

2. Within nanoseconds, your brain automatically makes an assumption about that behavior. In this critical moment, you have a choice to make.

3. One option is to go with that initial assumption. This is what reinforces your story and makes you feel closed off.

4. Create a more informed story.

5. This allows you and them to feel more open and curious...

6. And develop a shared understanding with the other person, which leads to more collaboration, innovation and commitment.

Pathway to Shared Understanding

Empowering Partners proprietary & copyrighted. All rights reserved.

Misunderstanding

Collaboration Innovation

6. Act out with Silence or Violence

6. Develop Shared Understanding

5. Feel Closed Off

5. Feel Open and Curious

4. Reinforce Story

4. Create a Story

3. Go with Assumption

3. Gather more information

2. Make an Assumption

1. See and Hear

BREATHE AND RELAX

As you've gained new experiences and insight in this chapter, take a contemplative moment or minute to breathe, relax and recognize yourself for showing up for this work. Navy SEALs use the following technique to stay calm and focused in tense situations. Try it: inhale to a count of 4; hold for 4; exhale for 4; hold for 4. Repeat. Try at least six rounds, more if necessary. Use this technique to take a break and rejuvenate during your day and/or when someone comes in hot with an aggressive remark, and you need to care for yourself before you respond.

THREE-DAY CHALLENGE

During the next three days observe, experience and practice noticing unconscious bias and its impact. Use your head, heart and hands to reflect and write in your journal:

Day 1: Today, observe what assumptions pop up about different people and circumstances.

1. What assumptions about people, groups or situations do you now notice coming up?
2. How do your assumptions reflect how you were raised in your culture?
3. How does knowing more about bias help you look at people and situations differently?

Day 2: Today, as you observe yourself and others, notice your own reactions associated with your assumptions.

1. What assumptions do you make about yourself?
2. How does it make you feel when people make assumptions about you?
3. What do you wish people would do instead of assuming?

Day 3: Today, watch the individual and collective impact of assumptions on people and groups.

1. What practice or policy in your organization or community inadvertently or intentionally leaves people feeling sidelined or silenced?
2. Who can help you determine who are the impacted stakeholders?
3. What cultural intelligence tool can you use to slow down decision-making and check the impact of those decisions on people?

CHAPTER 5:
EXPRESSING COMPASSION

When you show deep empathy toward others, their defensive
energy goes down, and positive energy replaces it.
That's when you can get more creative in solving problems.

- STEPHEN COVEY

In the middle of a conversation with another person, have you ever thought: "You just don't get it." Or, "You really don't understand me." It's so frustrating; we've all been in that position at one time or another. We've all been that other person, too – the one who really isn't listening. That was the case for Angela, a store manager of a retail chain.

After the workshop on empathy for the retail company, Angela came up to me before the next workshop got started. She told me she'd been having a hard time communicating with the younger people on staff. She said, "Your workshop on empathy for another person within their context got me thinking. I'd gotten so caught up in the day-to-day running of the store, it hadn't occurred to me that I wasn't really connecting with my employees. After the workshop last week, I over-heard two of my team members talking in the breakroom. I realized I really didn't know much about them. It made me wonder if that's why some of them get defensive when I need to correct them."

I said, "So, what did you discover?"

Angela said, "Just before closing that day, one of my particularly difficult employees and I got to talking. I really stopped and listened to him. I sat with him and even looked him in the eyes. He opened up about his struggles. Then, I shared a little bit about overcoming some challenges in my past. For the first time, I understood where he was coming from, and he understood me."

I said, "That's so cool. What happened?"

Angela said, "Well, since our talk, I've seen a change in his attitude: he's more understanding with his co-workers, and he's up for doing what I ask him to do now. Empathy helped us connect. He also doesn't let the small stuff get to him anymore. He's more productive. And the best part is he's nicer to me and the customers."

Angela saw an increase in productivity and engagement when she slowed down and took the opportunity to connect with her younger employee. She was able to appreciate this employee's perspective and change her behavior to show him genuine respect. That's cultural intelligence in action because cultural differences can show up across generations, too.

To help a person in your organization or community feel valued, heard, seen and engaged, you learned in the previous chapter to slow down and notice how your assumptions can block you from genuine connection. However, when a person opens up and shares vulnerably with you, like Angela's employee did, you may not know how to respond in a way that creates a connection. That's why, in this chapter, you'll learn how to express empathy for a person in their context.

Empathy is so important to an organization that it's the number one ability needed to work with people of different backgrounds and perspectives.

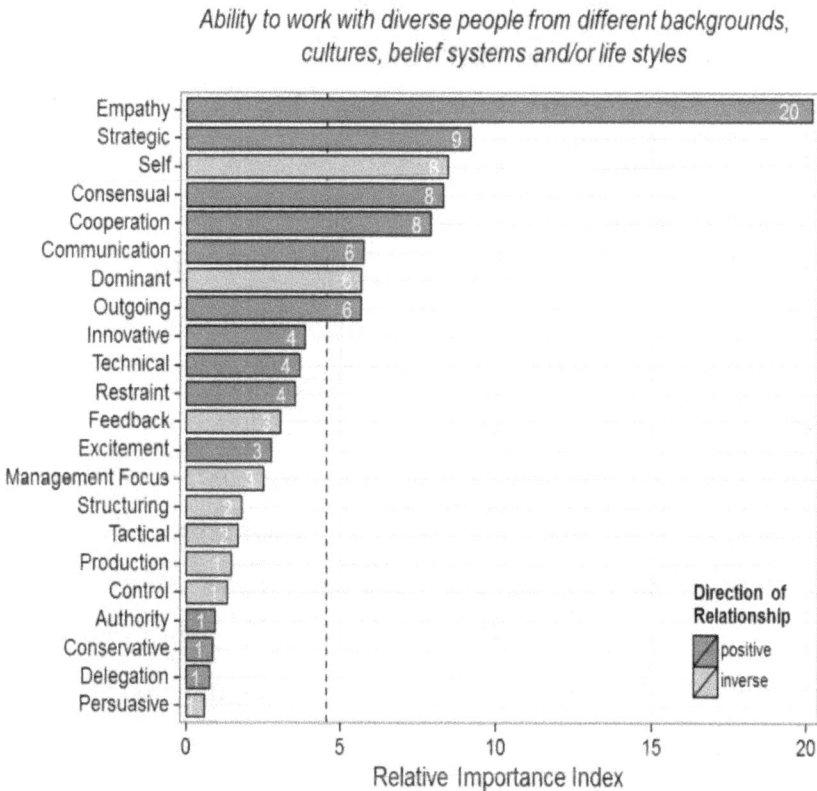

Ability to work with diverse people from different backgrounds, cultures, belief systems and/or life styles

Category	Relative Importance Index
Empathy	20
Strategic	9
Self	8
Consensual	8
Cooperation	8
Communication	6
Dominant	5
Outgoing	6
Innovative	4
Technical	4
Restraint	4
Feedback	3
Excitement	3
Management Focus	4
Structuring	2
Tactical	2
Production	1
Control	1
Authority	1
Conservative	1
Delegation	1
Persuasive	

Direction of Relationship
positive
inverse

Relative Importance Index

Credit: Research Management Group

WHAT EMPATHY IS

Empathy and sympathy are not the same (Brown, 2017). **Empathy** is recognizing emotion in another, feeling with the person and taking their perspective. It doesn't require that you've experienced the same situation they are going through. However, it does require courage, vulnerability and active listening to feel along with them. As a result, empathy fuels connection.

On the other hand, **sympathy** is trying to make something better for another person. With sympathy, you might say, "... at least," offer a silver lining or try to give them a solution. Because these responses don't acknowledge the person's feelings, it actually makes them feel more alone. As a result, sympathy drives disconnection.

Empathy is so important for connection because frustration and resentment can build within an organization when even one person doesn't feel valued, heard, seen or engaged. For example, a valued, veteran employee met successively with four different leaders in her organization concerning a set of issues out of her control that blocked her from being productive. None of the four leaders expressed empathy or worked to understand the issues and their impact on her. Feeling frustrated and alone, she felt she had no choice but to leave the organization. If just one of those leaders had taken the time to appreciate her frustration and express empathy, the company could have retained a valuable team member.

EMPATHY HAS ITS LIMITATIONS

Empathy is vital to productive relationships, but it's not enough. Empathy needs to be leveled up because it has its limitations. Empathy can be biased. Empathy tends to:

- Focus on our own circle of influence. It sometimes shines a light only on those we care about within our circle. For example, it's easy to care about your friends and their needs. It's much harder to muster up empathy for adversaries at work; it's easier to think they're getting their just desserts.

- Be influenced by preconceived ideas of what we think about a person, group or situation. For example, as a sales manager, it's easy to excuse my top salesperson for a family emergency, trusting they will make up for the lost time. However, it may be harder to feel empathy for a salesperson with an identical family emergency who has been dragging their feet and not making their sales numbers.

- Be shortsighted. It can be blind to future impacts and results of our behaviors. For example, a manager can provide a direct report with an office, desk, phone extension and computer but, without learning the employee's context and skill level, the employee may not be able to sell to customers.

- Favor one person over many people. An example overheard: "I care about what happens to my friend and coworker, especially when I hear or see sexism, because she is a great person and hard worker. But I am overwhelmed thinking about how to care for all the people of marginalized groups in our organization."

Knowing that empathy can be biased is the first step to leveling up to being even more productive with compassion. You need empathy because *feeling* empathy with another person is the first step to *being* compassionate. Compassion is not only feeling with a person, it also includes a tangible expression of care and concern for their suffering. Compassion also allows for some emotional distance or perspective; it's more deliberate, conscious and sustainable, and less likely to lead to burnout. Angela felt empathy and acted with compassion for her employee. That's what allowed the employee to become more engaged, committed and productive in their store.

Compassion involves three elements – noticing, feeling and responding to the other person.

Step 1: Notice

1. Notice the other's pain.
2. Slow down; check that you're safe.
3. Recognize your reaction and assumption.

Step 2: Feel

1. Feel your feelings and name them to yourself.
2. Imagine the other person's situation and how they feel.

Step 3: Respond

1. Respond by labeling the person's emotion. Use one of these beginning phrases:

   - It seems like you're [inspired].

   - It sounds like you're [confused].

   - It looks like you're [angry].

CULTURAL INTELLIGENCE TOOL

To demonstrate compassion for another person within their context:

1. Notice

2. Feel

3. Respond

Use one of these beginning neutral statements – "It seems like…", "It sounds like…" or "It looks like…" – to focus the conversation on the other person. These statements keep the encounter about them and help to create a connection. Making it about them is how you can help them feel valued, heard, seen and engaged.

It's important to note that you may have been trained to use I-statements when talking about feelings. To clarify, you use I-statements when you're talking about your *own* feelings, for example, "I feel angry when you [do such and such]…" Whereas you use neutral statements when you're talking about *their* feelings - "It sounds like you're [angry]."

PRO TIP: You can't genuinely express compassion for another until you've first expressed compassion for yourself. Self-acceptance is the foundation of cultural intelligence. By accepting your own humanity – all the broken and beautiful parts in there together – you'll have the bandwidth to see the humanity in others.

ATTITUDE OF COMPASSION

Underlying the compassion you demonstrate are three qualities – dignity, solidarity and accountability. **Dignity** is the inherent worth of every human being. **Solidarity** is a demonstration of unity in thoughts, words and actions, which produces a community of interest, objectives and standards. **Accountability** is taking responsibility individually and collectively for our words and actions and their impact on ourselves and others.

When you communicate with compassion and solidarity, you recognize the inherent dignity of another. When you need to reverse a previously unhelpful behavior that inadvertently ignored another's dignity, you can act with accountability.

CULTURAL INTELLIGENCE TOOL

To be seen to have dignity is an unspoken human yearning we all share. These five key elements and their correlating behaviors are what help people feel you see their inherent dignity.

1. Acceptance of Identity – rather than approaching people as inferior or superior, assume they have integrity.

2. Acknowledgment – give people your full attention; notice, feel and respond to their concerns and what they've been through.

3. Safety – put people at ease on two levels: a) physically, so they feel free from bodily harm and b) psychologically, so they feel free of concern about being shamed or humiliated.

4. Benefit of the doubt – treat people as trustworthy, start with the premise that others have good motives and are acting with integrity and doing the best they can within their circumstances, even if you don't yet completely understand where they're coming from.

5. Accountability – take responsibility individually and collectively for our words and actions and check your impact. If you have violated the dignity of another, appreciate their pain, apologize if needed and make a commitment to change hurtful behaviors.

These five elements of dignity are not apparent in this case study about Collette, a diligent boss, and Madison, one of her most dedicated nurses. After you read it, take a few minutes to digest the impact on people of an efficient but compassionless workplace.

CASE STUDY:
MANAGING WITHOUT COMPASSION

Collette could not understand why so many of her nurses were transferring to another location within the hospital system or just quitting altogether. She ran a tight ship; she treated everyone the same and everyone worked with precision, following the policies and procedures to a "T." They were nurses delivering life-saving medications with the potential to be lethal if handled incorrectly with their cancer patients; she understood uniformity and conformity to be critical.

Because of their excellence, they were often asked by the main hospital, to which they were a satellite, to be the first nursing team to test and implement new procedures. Collette was proud of how her team handled the opportunities and challenges. She just told them what the new policy or procedure was, and they did it – no questions asked. But just last Friday, one of the most dedicated nurses on Collette's team, Madison, quit on the spot with no notice, leaving the entire team short-handed. Collette huffed, "That's fine. We need team players." She got to where she was by being a stickler for the rules and delivering what she promised.

Madison loved being a nurse. Like many nurses, she was drawn to the job because it required compassion, helped others feel good and had no homework. She liked the fact that you come, do your shift well and go home to your family. But last Friday, Madison forgot all about why she loved her job. It had gotten where there was just too much homework. She and her teammates worked day and night for Collette, often bringing new procedure manuals home to study or train outside of normal work hours.

Things were getting out of hand

Madison felt certain Collette was so busy making a name for herself at corporate that she never noticed the team was bending over backwards, saving lives, working short-handed and often without breaks, staying late, doing more and more homework – all with no voice in Collette's ever-changing policies and procedures.

The stress was so overwhelming with life and work changes due to the pandemic heaped on top, career nurses who had worked at this location for 15-20+ years were transferring to other locations or a new hospital or just quitting. Every week the team was down by 1-3 nurses, making patient population-to-nurse ratios dangerously high.

Madison and the rest of the team knew many of Collette's procedures didn't work efficiently, but Collette did not work directly with patients to know the procedures were not workable and did not tolerate feedback. The team mostly hoped that this boss, like so many other ladder-climbing bosses, would be sucked out of their hair and into the corporate office soon.

Last Friday, when Madison saw Collette putting her on the following week's schedule, Madison reminded Collette she was on vacation that week. Madison and her husband Mike and two children had spent a year dreaming and planning their RV road trip through the Rocky Mountains. She had gotten the time off approved eight months ago. Plane tickets were purchased, the RV deposit made, campsites reserved and all kinds of gear purchased. Mike had gotten time off work and these were the only two weeks a year one kid or the other did not have a practice, game or recital. Besides, Madison was worn out – she needed this vacation.

When Collette said, "Madison, you do not have vacation time. You did not add it in the new time system when the time system switch was made last month," Madison lost it. Without saying a word (because, with Collette, what was the point?!) or consulting Mike, she walked to the break room, removed her belongings from her locker and marched right back up to Collette, handing over her ID card. While giving Collette some choice words about what Collette could do with *her* schedule, *her* new time system, *her* procedures and *her* job – because, Madison stated loud and clear, "Effective immediately I no longer work here and all that recognition you get at corporate, maybe it's time you realize it's a team effort that comes at a great cost to everyone but you."

Madison had never felt so good. Her health and well-being were worth as much as the patients she so diligently cared for and loved. She could not work one minute longer for someone who did not value her as an employee and a person.

What are the 5 C's™ of Collette and Madison's Story?

Take a few minutes to consider how the 5 C's™ were *not* applied in the case study about Collette and Madison:

- Curiosity
- Contemplation
- Courage
- Context
- Compassion

By managing an efficient but compassionless workplace, Collette lost a valued employee. It's clear Collette needs to learn how to lead with compassion if she wants to reverse attrition and ultimately save the organization time and money. But what about Madison? Could she use cultural intelligence to more effectively manage her task-oriented boss? That's exactly what a client of mine asked me in her executive coaching session, "How do I manage up?"

CASE STUDY:
HOW TO MANAGE UP

"I'd like to improve my relationship with my boss," said Kayla in her executive coaching session. Kayla is the Director of Services at her bank.

I said, "What's going on?"

Kayla said, "I don't know what to do about my boss, Linda. I had a great relationship with my old boss at my previous bank. We had a great connection and she had high standards, but I always knew where I stood with her."

I said, "Sounds like you had a solid relationship. [She nodded.] What prompted you to leave that bank, then?"

Kayla said, "There was no room for me to advance – I had to move on."

I said, "It must've been a tough decision to leave such a great boss."

Kayla said, "It was. Just recently, Linda told me I was being argumentative in a meeting with a vendor, but I was just asking questions to get a better understanding. Later on, she told me it wasn't my place to speak, I shouldn't have even been invited to the meeting. She should have been straight with me in the first place. She should have my back, like my old boss did."

I said, "How did that situation impact you?"

Kayla said, "I felt invisible, like I don't matter."

I said, "Feelings like that are legit. Our feelings can indicate a problem to solve. Question for you: Is there any chance you're holding up that old relationship as a standard for this new relationship?"

Kayla said, "I hadn't thought of that."

I said: "I get that you appreciate your old boss. Ok, just so I know, is there anything you like about Linda?

Kayla said, "Yes, she doesn't micromanage me."

I said, "That's cool. Because she's not involved in your day-to-day, that may indicate she doesn't know you well yet."

Kayla said, "That's true."

I said, "So what do *you* need?"

Kayla said, "I need her to have my back."

I said, "I get that. I also know you can't change her, but you *can* change you. But before you try to change you, it's important to give yourself some compassion. Cultural intelligence empowers people from the inside out. It's what enables you to accept a person and situation as they are and communicate with genuine respect to care for both you and them. You can't genuinely care for another until you've first cared for yourself."

"I continued, to care for you first, you can ask yourself these questions about the situation:

- How do I feel? Acknowledge your feelings. Being made to feel invisible hurts a soul. It takes courage to slow down, feel your feelings and hold them tenderly as you would a puppy.
- What do I need to care for me?
- What is mine to do in this situation?
- How can I create a win-win scenario?"

Kayla said, "That really helps. Now that I think about it, I need to connect with her. When she, another manager and I went out for drinks after work last week, we had a good rapport. But there wasn't a deeper connection that I have been longing for. I need her to really know me."

I said, "That's legitimate. What can you do to create a deeper connection?"

Kayla said: "I know that, if you want someone to do something for you, it can help to do it first. Ah, there's my opportunity: I can initiate more regular meetings with Linda so she knows more about what I do. I can share what's on my mind. Then I can learn more about what she needs."

I said, "That's it. By creating a regular flow of meaningful conversation, you're creating a win-win scenario for both of you. Closing that communication gap with compassion is you managing *up* with cultural intelligence."

What happened

A week later, I emailed Kayla to ask her how it was going. She said, "Linda and I had lunch on Tuesday, and we talked about this. That was the first time we've connected one-to-one in person in quite some time. It went really well. I'm happy with the direction we're headed. Thanks, Dr. Amy, for your help!"

CULTURAL INTELLIGENCE TOOL

To care for yourself in light of a challenging relationship, you can ask yourself and reflect on these questions one at a time:

- How do I feel?
- What do I need to care for me?
- What is mine to do in this situation?
- How can I create a win-win scenario?

What are the 5 C's™ of Kayla's Story?

Take a few minutes to consider how the 5 C's™ were applied in the case study about Kayla:

- Curiosity
- Contemplation
- Courage
- Context
- Compassion

With cultural intelligence, you begin to see people's problems as opportunities. You recognize that, yes, these steps take time, compassion and tenacity, but good things happen in the process. Kayla did have to slow down, honor her feelings and needs, and muster the courage to discover more compassion for herself. But that's what ultimately gave her the bandwidth and power to create a win-win for herself and her boss.

If it isn't obvious yet, compassion isn't something you just have; it's something you grow. As you engage with another person, it's important to keep in mind that compassion is about understanding the circumstances from the other person's perspective. When you show compassion for them in their context, it does not indicate agreement; it only indicates understanding. That shared understanding is what creates genuine connection, engagement and commitment.

CONVERSATION PARTNER EXERCISE

You'll need your Conversation Partner to do this "One Speaker, One Listener" exercise together. Remember to use the steps for compassion – notice, feel and respond.

This is how it works. In this activity:

1. The Speaker shares one high and one low from the previous week.
2. The Listener hears the speaker.
3. When the Speaker finishes sharing, the Listener labels the emotion(s) heard.
4. Then, switch roles and repeat the exercise.

When you're the Speaker:

- Share your story (2-3 minutes).
- Notice your own feelings as you speak.
- Notice if you feel vulnerable speaking.

When you're the Listener:

- Notice hidden assumptions that show up that might distract you from really listening.
- Notice your own feelings as you spot the Speaker's emotion.
- Notice how you want to problem-solve (but don't).
- Allow the Speaker to finish sharing before you label their emotion.

PRO TIP: When you practice compassion, you come to appreciate the other person's perspective and experience. That emotional connection with another person communicates solidarity. Solidarity in personal and professional relationships is what creates a sense of belonging and commitment to the work and organization.

BREATHE AND RELAX

Practicing cultural intelligence, especially the component of compassion, can use a lot of energy. A contemplative walk, also known as a mindful walk, reduces stress, improves focus, enhances your mood, and allows you to appreciate the present moment. While you walk, inhale deeply and slowly through your nose and exhale through your mouth. Try to inhale for 3 to 4 steps, and then exhale for the next 3 to 4 steps. Repeat this pattern of breathing while walking at a relaxed pace for at least 5 minutes. Though countercultural to care for your own well-being, taking time like this to care for you is what gives you the bandwidth to genuinely care for others. This is similar to when a flight attendant instructs you to put your own oxygen mask on first before you help others.

THREE-DAY CHALLENGE

During the next three days, observe, experience and practice compassion in your organization or community. Use your head, heart and hands to reflect and write in your journal:

Day 1: Today, look for examples of compassion in action.

1. Where do you see compassion demonstrated in your workplace and where is it missing?
2. How did the compassion expressed change the dynamic of the conversation you observed?
3. How does Minimization deter you from expressing compassion to yourself?

Day 2: Today, observe how compassion makes you and others feel.

1. What are the situations where you wish someone had expressed more compassion toward you?

2. What are the situations where you inadvertently minimized another person and wished you'd expressed more compassion?

3. How does reflecting on and feeling compassion change how you look at yourself and others?

Day 3: Today, watch where compassion is needed individually and collectively.

1. What practice or policy in your organization or community inadvertently or intentionally leaves people feeling sidelined or silenced?

2. Who can help you identify the impacted stakeholders?

3. What cultural intelligence tools can you use to take a first step so that those stakeholders feel valued, heard, seen and engaged?

CHAPTER 6:
RECOGNIZING OUR CULTURE

I don't like that man. I must get to know him better.

-ABRAHAM LINCOLN

It can be hard to feel compassion when you don't know a person and their circumstances. In a workshop I was giving, a White CEO told his team that reports of Tyre Nichols' death barely hit his radar screen. It hadn't occurred to him to discuss it with anyone – at least not until he saw how much Nichols' death affected his Black wife. She told him the news of the tragedy lit up her phone with texts from family and friends. He said he was stunned by the difference in their respective communities' levels of response to the death.

The CEO realized he wouldn't have known the impact of the tragedy on the Black community if it hadn't been for the relationship with his wife. It's not uncommon for people of the dominant culture in any community, organization or country to be culturally blind to the system – the cultural container – and the way it affects them and people of underrepresented communities.

You don't see the cultural container if you haven't: built authentic relationships with people outside your culture, considered the impact of the dominant culture on marginalized people or actively developed awareness of the other's cultural characteristics through relationships, education and travel. It's like being right-handed in a right-handed world. The system works in your favor, so you don't notice that, for left-handed people, the desk doesn't support their writing arm, the notebook's spiral gets in the way and the scissors don't work in the "wrong" hand.

See the blindness

To see the implicit systems that influence the way we think, feel, talk and act, you need to recognize a particular mental model in play within the culture: cultural blindness, also called Minimization. The problem with having so much of humanity stuck in this default mode is that minimizing and ignoring others' differing experiences creates an environment in which people tend to focus on what everyone has in common and assume others' experiences are like their own. This inadvertently minimizes, dismisses and marginalizes those of underrepresented groups. **Cultural blindness** is the belief that one's own culture and norms are universally applicable, overlooking the opportunities other cultures have to offer. This perception can be well-intentioned but is definitely flawed – limiting productivity, engagement and commitment.

Members of the non-dominant culture groups tend to be very aware of the system but go along to get along (minimize too) because they are not in positions of power and, therefore, can be hesitant or fearful to speak up or out. This dismissiveness of people's humanity is often demoralizing and dangerous for people of non-dominant groups in any organization.

How this happens

People's individual actions don't come out of a void. They are a reflection of a larger system, the dominant culture surrounding them. Dr. Edward Deming (1900–1993), a renowned management consultant, argued that 94% of problems are caused by the system, not the individual. The problem of cultural blindness, then, is not that anybody is inherently evil but that people have an inherited ignorance of the system. The good news is if ignorance is the fundamental problem, it's a fixable problem.

The antidote to cultural blindness is to become more self-aware of the systems that influence us, which makes us less likely to perpetuate them. To upend minimization, people of the dominant culture can become aware of their culture and its impact on themselves and others, as well as recognize that each person's experience is just one of many cultural patterns.

Who I learned from

The danger is very real for my friend Kimberly St. Clair. As an African American mom, she is particularly worried about her son, who is on the autism spectrum. She can't anticipate how he'll behave under the pressure of a traffic stop. She was so worried that she developed a tool and curriculum called Doc Dash, designed to keep civilians and officers safe during traffic stops.

Because, statistically, people from dominant cultural groups are unaware of systems and their impact on others, they don't necessarily have the practice, skills and vocabulary to talk and learn with people who have been historically silenced. That's probably why so often, after a tragedy like Tyre Nichols' death, Kimberly is asked by her White friends what they can do to help.

It's no one person's fault how the system works; however, to quote Maya Angelou, "...when you know better, do better." To upend the cultural blindness in any organization, community or society, it's important for people of the dominant culture to become more and more aware of the cultural characteristics that are helping and hindering relationships.

CULTURAL INTELLIGENCE TOOL

To upend cultural blindness, you can:

1. Educate yourself about the characteristics of your dominant culture and its influence on how you think, feel, talk and act.

2. Learn how the dominant culture impacts people of historically underrepresented groups and can block access to legal, financial, educational, mental and physical well-being.

3. Lift up voices that all too often go unheard for greater authenticity, safety and collaboration for everyone. For more details, you can study *How to Be an Ally* in the Appendix.

CULTURAL CHARACTERISTICS

Cultural characteristics are features like the beliefs, behaviors, material objects and values, typically shared by a specific group of people that are used to better understand a person in their context, to connect with them. Cultural characteristics are different from stereotypes, though.

Stereotypes are based on features like beliefs, behaviors, material objects and values typically shared by a group of people that are used with the intention to label, shame and limit a person or group. For example, "all women like to shop" or "all men love sports."

Cultural characteristics are used with the intention of learning more about other people – to better understand them in their context and develop a genuine relationship. For example, Americans tend to be more task-oriented, while Spaniards tend to be more relationship-oriented. Knowing these cultural characteristics helps you be more compassionate because if you're an American talking with a Spaniard, you'll know to slow down and share something about yourself before jumping into work-related talk.

> **PRO TIP:** Learning the characteristics of the dominant culture empowers you to be aware of what's driving your thoughts, feelings, words and actions. It also empowers you to be aware of its impact on dominant and non-dominant cultural group members.

Learning about cultural characteristics allows you to give a person dignity even though they're different from you. Cultural characteristics are not right/wrong or good/bad; each culture has its upsides and downsides. However, most of us are biased by familiarity and tend to think our culture is the best, just as the CEO was at the beginning of this chapter. As a result, a person's culture can be a sensitive topic, similar to talking about someone's mother. So often, there is a protective instinct for the culture you consider your own. While it may be easy to discuss the faults of your own culture, so often others may not talk about your culture without it feeling like an insult. I've noticed this playing out with our French family. I may be critical of American culture at times but feel defensive when they make such remarks.

Though it may be risky, I'll name a few characteristics of dominant American culture that can keep us from genuinely connecting with another person if we're not aware. They include:

- **Individualism** is prioritizing the needs of the individual over the needs of the group.
- **Competitiveness** is a binary separation of people and groups into one winner with the rest losing or made to feel less-than.
- **Perfectionism** leads people and groups to be judgmental and identify what is wrong with themselves and others based on standards outside of ourselves.
- **Urgency** is when time is viewed as linear and limited; faster is better.
- **Task-oriented** is the ability to show up on time and complete tasks reliably and in a timely fashion. It can be a problem when a task is prioritized over the needs or feelings of ourselves and others.

HOW TRUST GROWS ACROSS CULTURE

Some of the most task-oriented cultures in the world are the United States, Canada, Netherlands, Denmark, Germany, and Australia. In such task-oriented cultures, trust is built on being accountable, pleasant, consistent and reliable. Whereas countries like Brazil, Mexico, Saudi Arabia, Nigeria, India and China are some of the most relationship-oriented cultures in the world. In relationship-oriented cultures, trust is built when you relax, laugh together and share on a personal level. In fact, they often won't want to do business with you until they've had "three cups of tea." This adage is based on an old Pakistani proverb that describes the progression of relationships through the act of sharing cups of tea. The proverb states that the first cup of tea is shared with a stranger, the second with a friend, and the third with family.

Trust is a vital element of doing business anywhere in the world. So it's important to know these two types of trust and how they grow. In a task-oriented culture, trust comes from the head and arises from confidence in someone's skills and their reliability. You work together and rely on another to complete tasks, follow directions and check in when help is needed. This type of trust is transactional, relying on repeated actions and less on emotional connection. In a relationship-oriented culture, trust comes from the heart and arises from emotional feelings of connection through talking, laughing and experiencing things together. Being together, you reach a level of comfort that leads to closeness, empathy, shared vulnerability and camaraderie. This type of trust is relational, based on connection and shared experience.

You can often see a combination of these two types of trust in your circle of family or friends. Think of one person in particular that you trust. Consider what they say and do that leads you to trust them. Then, identify the kind of trust-building that describes their behavior. It's likely to be a combination of both kinds of trust.

In a diverse work environment, use your head to focus on being accountable, reliable, consistent and pleasant. Also, use your heart to focus on building a relationship with colleagues and clients by listening, getting to know their story and affirming their feelings and experiences, even though they may be different from your own. Employing a combination of being reliable *and* relational is how to most effectively build trust across cultures in your organization and community.

CULTURAL INTELLIGENCE TOOL

To build trust across cultures, use both your

- Head to focus on being accountable, reliable, consistent and pleasant.

- Heart to focus on building a relationship with colleagues and clients through talking, laughing and experiencing things together.

No doubt, there are times when it's necessary to be task-oriented. You need to get stuff done. The beauty of having cultural intelligence is you recognize that it's the context that matters – there are times when you need to focus on the other person or yourself, and there are times when the task must take priority. In Abby's case, she has to prioritize the relationship to do her job as a journalist well.

CASE STUDY:
HOW A JOURNALIST BUILDS TRUST

"What do you do to capture the stories you do from people with such diverse perspectives?" I asked Abby, a journalist for a media outlet based in New York City.

Abby said, "People don't always initially trust me. But that doesn't mean the story shouldn't be told. I have to demonstrate I'm worthy of trust.

I said, "That's not an easy task. I've discovered that after years of being belittled under the system of minimization, people of color, women and those who are differently abled may hesitate to speak up for fear of retaliation, misrepresentation, social isolation or job loss even when asked to speak up."

Abby said, "That's true. There are some stories that I have to take the time to build a genuine relationship before the person opens up. As a White person, I have extra work to do – particularly with people from under-represented groups who are unaccustomed to being heard. I have to create a space where they feel safety and trust. It's worth the investment of time, though, because I get to meet and talk with people I never would have known before, and our media outlet gets more in-depth reporting."

I said, "How do you gain people's trust so you can capture more of the story?"

Abby said, "It takes some courage. I cover stories domestically and internationally. I've discovered most people around the world are not White like me. We're actually in the minority, globally. But because of our historical context, I can be perceived as threatening to some people. So, I've learned to be a bit vulnerable and straight-up own my whiteness. I also know I can be blind to what it's like for other people. So, I say, 'Because of my whiteness, I'm not always aware of what it's like for others. Would you mind telling me your story so that I can share it with people who need to know?' This is just me owning my humanity, which people seem to appreciate."

I said, "How do they respond to your question?"

Abby said, "When I ask that question, I've learned to allow for different reactions. For some people, being asked questions by a White woman can be upsetting; it can trigger emotional trauma. Whereas for other people, the same question can be affirming for them; they're so grateful to finally have a voice. If someone is hurt by my question, I just back off and affirm their feelings. I can then redirect the conversation to a safer topic or stop altogether. But in most cases, if I show compassion for people within their context, people want to share their stories. And with the cultural intelligence I express and the trust I develop, I can capture an in-depth story."

What are the 5 C's™ of Abby's Story?

Take a few minutes to consider how the 5 C's™ apply in the case study about Abby:

- Curiosity
- Contemplation
- Courage
- Context
- Compassion

These are the five elements of cultural intelligence that help you successfully navigate a conversation with someone who has a different perspective or background.

> **PRO TIP:** With trust established, people with domestic and international differences tend to more easily forgive cultural missteps or personal misunderstandings. That connection creates more openness, authenticity and loyalty between people and with their organization in the long run.

CONVERSATION PARTNER EXERCISE

You'll need your Conversation Partner to do this "One Speaker, One Listener" exercise together. With your conversation partner, share a time when being task-oriented got in the way of being present with someone. This is an opportunity to use your compassion to connect with your partner.

Here's how it works. In this activity:

1. The speaker shares with the conversation partner their experience of being task-oriented rather than relationship-oriented.

2. The listener hears the speaker.

3. When the speaker finishes sharing, the listener labels the emotion(s) heard.

4. Then, the two switch roles and repeat the exercise.

GUIDELINES

When you're the speaker:

- Share your stories (2-3 minutes each).
- Notice your own feelings as you speak.
- Notice if you feel vulnerable speaking.

When you're the listener:

- Notice hidden assumptions that show up which might distract you from really listening.
- Notice your own feelings as you spot the speaker's emotion.
- Notice how you want to problem solve (but don't do that).
- Allow the speaker to finish sharing before you label their emotion.

BREATHE AND RELAX

Contemplative practices emphasize self-awareness, self-regulation, and/or self-inquiry to bring about more well-being for you, your family and everyone in your sphere of influence. Without self-awareness, there is often an incongruence between your feelings and your non-verbal communication. As a result, you're unable to see how your actions impact the people around you.

To become more self-aware, take a moment or minute three times a day to notice and name your feelings. If that's too much, record a physical sensation in your body. For example, S.T.O.P. at 8 a.m., 11 a.m. and 3 p.m., feel your feelings or the sensations and make a note of them in your journal. Are you mad, sad, glad or scared? Write just one word. If you can take an extra moment, record what prompted that feeling. Taking time for you three times a day is an act of compassion. As you care for yourself, you'll have more bandwidth and be able to more genuinely care for the people around you. This creates more collaboration, commitment and cohesiveness in your home, workplace and community.

THREE-DAY CHALLENGE

Over the next three days, you have a chance to observe and experience how people from different backgrounds and cultures build trust. Use your head, heart and hands to reflect on and write in your journal:

Day 1: Today, look for examples of our dominant and non-dominant cultural characteristics.

1. When do you see a task-orientation help build trust and productivity?

2. When do you see a relationship-orientation help build trust and productivity?

3. When do you need both a task- and relationship-orientation to build trust and productivity?

Day 2: Today, take the opportunity to notice your reaction to task- and relationship-oriented behavior.

1. When do you feel judged based solely on your reliability, skills and accomplishments?

2. In what situations do you wish a colleague would take the time to build heart trust?

3. How can your feelings inform what you know about a colleague?

Day 3: Today, watch for times that relationship-building could benefit your organization or community.

1. What practice or policy in your department, organization or community inadvertently or intentionally sidelines or silences people and diminishes productivity?

2. Who are the impacted stakeholders of that practice or policy?

3. What cultural intelligence tools can you use to take a first step that builds a relationship with the impacted stakeholders?

CHAPTER 7:
SEEKING SHARED UNDERSTANDING

*Probably the most important connection builder is simple
but active and intentional listening. It is simple because it gets
to the most basic need in life. People want to be known and
understood. You cannot lead them to another place if they do
not feel like you understand the place they are in.*

– HENRY CLOUD

Another cultural characteristic many of us in the West experience is a
sense of urgency. That's a normal feeling when you live in a task-oriented society. We all feel those time constraints at one time or another.

Because you feel hurried, you can default to reflexively fixing
or correcting other people's problems without listening first. This is
particularly true for people who identify with the dominant culture.
Rather than being a *listener*, you tend to be a *speaker*. Rather than being
a *learner*, you tend to be a *knower*. This reflex can inadvertently hurt
working relationships, particularly in multicultural environments.

To counteract this cultural default, take a moment or a minute and apply S.T.O.P. It's in that quiet you'll discover you can adopt this attitude of listening and learning. It'll help you shed the cultural tendency to railroad past the other person and empower them to figure out what is the next best step for themselves within their own context. This also takes the pressure and responsibility off you to figure out the right fix for them. The best part is that listening actively allows you to connect instead of correct and ultimately allows you to forge more authentic and productive relationships.

More authentic and productive relationships are what Mary, the CEO of a credit union, discovered when she started listening to understand. After a workshop, Mary had a question for me. She told me she regularly holds listening circles to ensure that her employees feel valued. And she also regularly surveys the employees' attitudes about work. But at one point, Mary got so overwhelmed by all the problems she heard, she stopped holding the listening circles. And the following month's survey scores dropped. So she started holding the listening circles again. And the following month's survey scores went back up. Mary, however, was still overwhelmed by all the problems. She said, "I'm at a loss about what to do."

I said, "I get it. You want to show compassion for your employees but end up feeling helpless that you can't solve their problems. That's especially hard for people in leadership." I asked Mary if I could share a story with her. She nodded.

The story

I said, "One Sunday, a badly beaten woman came into church. Though I'm white, my family and I attend an African American church, which means we sometimes have different ways of responding to situations. I tend to be more task-oriented, while my fellow church members tend to be more relationship-oriented. The lady needed help; my first reaction was to figure out a fix for her problem.

"Quickly sizing up the situation, I decided her problems were more than our church could help with. So I started heading toward my phone to see who we might call for help. That's when a church elder, Darlene, called me back. I was pretty overwhelmed by the suffering I was seeing but resigned to the idea that maybe I could learn something here. While another church member got the visitor a cup of water and a protein bar, Darlene invited her to sit down just outside the sanctuary. Darlene and I then sat down by the woman's side and just held her.

"There in the hall, she just cried and eventually started to share her story of trauma. For fifteen minutes or so, we listened and heard her all the way out. We affirmed her feelings. Darlene rocked her and whispered encouragement after she told her story. I could only imagine what she and her children had been through all those months. After a while, another elder came with some fresh clothes and took her to get changed. While she was in the ladies' room, I went to the front of the church to tell my family where I'd been. When I turned back around, the lady was there in the back pew, standing up, smiling and dancing with the congregation."

I continued, "Later that day, I called Darlene to learn how she knew what to do. How was she not overwhelmed by the situation? Darlene said she didn't know what to do either. But she did know that if we showed compassion, the woman would figure out the next best step for herself. Darlene reminded me that neither she nor I were going to save the lady. The best we could do at that moment was actively listen to her."

I said to Mary, "How does that example land on you?"

Mary's response

Mary was quiet and reflective. Then she said, "I'd had the impression that I was supposed to solve all of my employees' problems. This takes a lot of pressure off."

I said, "Yes, that's pretty normal. In hierarchical contexts like your workplace, people of the dominant culture often unconsciously feel and act as if they know all the answers. Because people of the dominant culture tend to inadvertently be a *knower*, they don't listen well and reflexively try to fix the other person's problem. But as you shift into being a learner and listener, you're off the hook. By listening actively and responding with compassion within the learning circles, you're providing the headspace for your employees to figure out their own next best step. That's culturally intelligent leadership."

Mary said, "I appreciate that. What a relief. I'd much rather empower them to come up with their own solutions. This takes a lot of pressure off me and puts the problem solving back on the person who can really do something about it. Thank you."

What are the 5 C's™ of Mary's story?

Take a few minutes to consider how the 5 C's™ apply in the case study about Mary:

- Curiosity
- Contemplation
- Courage
- Context
- Compassion

By listening, you can help the speaker discover their own solution, which lets you off the hook from having to get it right or, if your solution is wrong, from being the one to blame. By listening, you also help the speaker feel valued and heard. Feeling less alone, they experience solidarity, which opens up the space for them to bump into their own next best step.

WHAT LISTENING IS

In U.S. schools, the focus is on teaching students to write, read and maybe speak, with little to no focus on listening. And yet, on the average day, we spend almost half of our time listening.

	TAUGHT	USED
Writing	Most	9%
Reading	Some	16%
Speaking	Little	30%
Listening	Least	45%

Think back to those days in school for a moment. When a teacher said to you, "Listen to me," what behaviors were they looking for? Typically, they were asking you to keep your mouth and body still, use eye contact and potentially nod or say, "Uh huh." That's **passive listening**.

CULTURAL INTELLIGENCE TOOL

Use passive listening behaviors to show that you're listening:

- Looks like eye contact, a quiet body except for some nodding.
- Sounds like "Uh huh," "Okay" or "Hmmm."

Passive listening shows respect because it allows the speaker to be heard without interruption. However, it doesn't require the listener to really pay attention to what's being said. Because you may not really be attending to what's being said, you can totally fake passive listening. For example, while a colleague is talking, you can totally be thinking about your grocery list, and they probably wouldn't even know.

The reason you have time to think about your grocery list is because the average speaker speaks 150-200 words per minute, while the average listener thinks 500-800 words per minute.

Rather than think about your grocery list, though, you may want to take the opportunity to create a genuine connection. If so, you can use those extra words you're thinking to understand what the speaker is saying. You're using that time to be prepared to paraphrase the content and/or feeling of what is being said. That's active listening.

Active listening is listening and responding with body language that looks and sounds like passive listening while also paying close attention to what the speaker is saying so you can paraphrase the content and/or feeling after they've finished. This technique is used to help the listener and speaker arrive at a shared understanding. It's important to note that **paraphrasing** is using your own words to say back what you heard the speaker said and the feeling they expressed to ensure a shared understanding.

CULTURAL INTELLIGENCE TOOL

Use active listening behaviors to develop a shared understanding with the other person:

- Looks like passive listening.
- Sounds like paraphrasing the content and/or feeling of what was just said.

Paraphrasing is not parroting what was said. Parroting exactly what was said can be annoying and off-putting to the speaker and shut down the conversation. It has the opposite effect of active listening.

Use active listening to ensure a person feels valued, heard, seen and engaged. Active listening involves three stages – hearing, paraphrasing and seeking.

Step 1: Hear Them Out

Active listening uses the same words and actions as passive listening. The difference is, when you're actively listening, you're hearing the speaker out and preparing to paraphrase back to them what they've said. Use eye contact, keep your body quiet except when you nod to show you're paying attention and say, "Uh huh" and "Okay." Let them finish talking. Don't interrupt, ask questions or offer a solution.

In this chapter's story, Mary was only passively listening to her employees because she was preparing to offer a solution rather than listening to understand and paraphrase. In the earlier chapter, Nurse Collette was not listening passively or actively. She was so focused on her tasks that she couldn't hear the stress and burnout she was causing that drove out her employee.

Step 2: Paraphrase the Content and Feeling of What Was Said

To paraphrase the content and feeling of what the speaker just said, notice their emotion. If possible, feel with them to appreciate what they're going through. To sound more genuine, paraphrase and reflect back to the speaker their emotion. Respond with compassion. Start by naming the emotions you heard with a phrase that starts:

- It seems like you're [angry].
- It sounds like you're [exhausted].
- It looks like you're [inspired].

CULTURAL INTELLIGENCE TOOL

When you're talking about your own feelings, use I-statements, like "I feel angry." Or, "I feel so happy." When you're talking about other people's feelings and don't want to sound presumptive, use more neutral statements like, "It sounds like you're angry." Or, "It seems like you're inspired."

For example, a bank teller says in an angry tone to her bank manager, "I will never wait on that customer again! She has no idea how hard my job is."

The Bank manager responds with compassion: "That customer must have been so rude. It sounds like you're super angry."

Bank teller: "You bet I'm angry!"

The Bank manager paraphrases: "Don't blame you. That's terrible!"

Bank teller: "Yeah, it really was." She takes a deep breath.

To make speakers feel valued, seen and heard, listeners may need to label the speaker's emotions several times to validate their feelings. Once the speaker takes a deep breath, sighs in relief, or is talking in a normal tone of voice and sounds more like themselves, you can move on to the next stage.

Step 3: Seek Understanding

When a person sounds more like themselves and they drop into silence, you can use questions like these to better understand and appreciate their context:

- May I ask you a question? (Ask if you can ask.)
- What happened that made you feel [upset]? (Seek understanding.)
- How does that land on you? (Check your impact.)

For example, once the Bank teller felt valued and heard, she took a deep breath and then calmly said, "I am used to rude customers, but the language this person used really pushed my buttons. It was so racist."

Bank manager: "What happened to you?"

Bank teller: "She said, 'I know it's your siesta time, but could you please get a move on?!'"

Bank manager paraphrased again: "Ouch! That hurts. I'm so sorry she said such a thing. Can I ask you a question? (The teller nodded.) Would you like to put our heads together and come up with ways to slow down and respond to this type of remark with savvy and cultural intelligence? We need to set boundaries to protect you and take care of that client without condoning their behavior."

Bank teller: "I'd appreciate that."

When a person like the Bank teller feels affirmed and understood, they have the capacity to shift from defensiveness and into problem-solving mode. You might ask, "What are some ways you'd like to handle a remark like that in the future?" Using our cultural intelligence training, how can we create a win-win – so that boundaries are set with compassion, and both parties feel seen and valued? Ideally, they'll name their own next best step or solution. Or maybe there is no apparent or immediate solution. In those instances, we can be present with the person and honor their feelings. This can help them feel less alone because someone is in their corner and isn't trying to fix them.

CULTURAL INTELLIGENCE TOOL

To actively listen and demonstrate compassion for another person in their context:

1. Hear them out.
2. Paraphrase the content and feeling of what was said.
3. Seek understanding.

COMPASSION INCLUDES ACCOUNTABILITY

With some people, active listening seems almost impossible. It's hard to actively listen and feel with a person who consistently sounds victimized, acts like a jerk, cries wolf or manipulates to serve only themselves.

It's easy to get sidetracked in these cases – thinking the unproductive behavior or false narrative is the person rather than their behavior. In these cases, you can still use active listening and demonstrate compassion while holding yourself and them accountable for productive behavior. You can demonstrate compassion because you: know there is a root cause driving their unproductive behavior and need to set clear boundaries for words and actions that contribute to a productive environment and cohesive culture.

Tools like a Performance Improvement Plan (PIP) can help. A PIP is a formal process used by employers to address employee under-performance, outlining specific areas for improvement, setting achievable goals and providing a time frame for achievement, with clear consequences to meet expectations. In this case study, Patricia used her cultural intelligence and a PIP to set up boundaries and the employee for success.

CASE-STUDY:
ACTIVE LISTENING LEADS TO ACTION

In her executive coaching session, Patricia, the Vice President of Human Resources of the hospital group, complained about their in-house counsel. He was all too often off-task and off-putting in leadership team meetings. She said, "When he attends a meeting in person, he whispers to his neighbor about others in the room, scrolls through his phone and doesn't contribute to the conversation. Sometimes, he attends by video call, even though he's right down the hall in his office. And we all know he's in the office because we can hear him talking. The thing is, when it's time for him to perform his job or the topic of the meeting is about his area, he's exceptional."

When she raised the issue about his behavior, the lawyer dismissed her. She said, "Not only has he made no effort to improve, he has since been trying to goad me in the leadership team meetings by clearly whispering to colleagues about me."

As she spoke, I didn't interrupt and heard her all the way out. When she finished talking, I said, "It sounds like you're exhausted."

Patricia said, "I am. I don't know what to do."

I said, "That's got to be tough to have a powerful person actively dismiss and undermine your vital role in the hospital."

Patricia said, "It's so tough." Then she took a deep breath. That was my cue that I could shift to seeking understanding.

I said, "May I ask you a question?" [She nodded.] "This sounds heavy and hard. Do you want me to listen and be with you in this, or would you like to problem solve?" (Another way of saying this is, "Would you like to be heard or helped at this time?")

Patricia said, "I want to problem solve."

I said, "You've already named specific unproductive behaviors. That's half the work right there. That's also the beginning of a Performance Improvement Plan, or PIP. Let's take the next step. What behaviors would you like to see instead?

Patricia said, "I'd like him to be productive and contribute to meetings."

I said, "What are the specific behaviors you need? Or, what does that look and sound like?"

Patricia said, "He needs to silence and put down his phone, look at the person who's talking, paraphrase people's ideas and then contribute ideas that are on the task at hand."

Together we determined the timeframe for improvement and got it all into the PIP.

What happened?

The next time we spoke, Patricia told me that the behavior-specific structure of the PIP gave her and her CEO the language they needed to set clear expectations for behavior and lay out a timeline for growth.

She said, "Thank you for giving me the space to feel and think through to next best steps. I knew what I needed to do, but I was so upset I just didn't know how to get started. Thank you for listening. You helped me shift from reacting to his dismissive behavior to responding thoughtfully about what the CEO and I could do to bring about the needed change."

I said, "You're totally welcome."

Patricia said, "This is not the kind of leadership training where someone is telling you how you should be or lead. You're doing leadership training that allows me to be my genuine self. Over these last few months, you've helped me lead in a way that's meaningful, particularly for me and my style. You're using cultural intelligence to help me develop mine. Thank you!"

What are the 5 C's™ of Patricia's Story?

Take a few minutes to consider how the 5 C's™ apply in the case study about Patricia:

- Curiosity
- Contemplation
- Courage
- Context
- Compassion

PRO TIP: Attempting to use logic or to argue with someone who is already upset just pushes them away. Trying to convince anyone of anything creates disconnection. Rather than correct, use active listening to create connection, consensus and collaboration

DETERMINE YOUR LISTENING GOAL

To empower Patricia to lead in a way that was meaningful for her and her style, I had to listen to understand her needs within her context. This is the goal of cultural intelligence: to listen for understanding. If you're not self-aware and intentional about your listening, you can get caught up in the dominant cultural tendency to act from urgency and shift into listening to be right, listening to speak or not really listening at all.

CULTURAL INTELLIGENCE TOOL

There are four different approaches to listening. To create connection with another person, go with #1.

1. Listening for understanding.
2. Listening to be right.
3. Listening to speak.
4. Not listening.

Not listening is a problem. Across industries, employers are concerned about retention and engagement. But rather than take the time to investigate the true causes of attrition, too many companies jump to well-intentioned quick fixes that fall flat. For example, they bump up pay or financial perks without making the effort to listen and strengthen the relational ties among colleagues and between staff and employers. This leaves an employee feeling invisible, as if their work is strictly a transactional relationship rather than one involving genuine appreciation. That was the case for Diana.

CASE STUDY:
ATTRITION TO APPRECIATION

Diana, a mid-level manager and long-time, respected member of her organization, called to give me an update. Diana said, "Do you remember my old boss and the trouble I was having?"

I said: "I do."

Diana said, "Dr. Amy, I tried to shove her abusive words to the back of my mind. I avoided looking for another job for months because I was exhausted from the 60-hour weeks my boss required I put in. She kept me up some nights with questions until 10 or 11 p.m. Then the next morning, she would call and ask why something wasn't done, knowing full well that, after the call, I'd gone to bed and had to get the kids off to school before starting work. To make things worse, if I ever made an error, she documented it in an email to the entire executive team. The last straw came when I was on vacation at Disney World with my family. She called with a question and fully expected an informed response on the spot. I gave my two weeks' notice right then.

"But you know most of that. The reason I called is to tell you about my new boss. She's the kind of boss you were teaching us to be in your training, Dr. Amy. Her leadership is awesome – I'd love to brag about her!"

I said, "Awesome. Tell me. What does she do and say that makes her such a good boss?"

Diana said, "Rhonda gives me public praise. When emails go out to the corporate attorney to check their work, Rhonda credits me for a job well done.

"Rhonda meets with me every other week to follow up on projects. When I meet with her, she gives me her full attention, like I'm the most important person in the world at that moment. Her affirmation, questions and tone encourage me to do the talking. I appreciate how she holds me accountable and gives me the runway to accomplish my tasks as long as I keep her in the loop. She asks me questions similar to what you taught us to ask our direct reports:

- 'What have you accomplished?'
- 'What's your next step?'
- 'How can I assist you?'"

CULTURAL INTELLIGENCE TOOL

In weekly or bi-weekly meetings, leaders can hold their direct reports compassionately accountable by asking three empowering questions:

- "What have you accomplished?"
- "What's your next step?"
- "How can I assist you?"

I asked, "How does she show her appreciation?"

Diana said, "She uses words that focus on creating a connection, like:

- 'Thank you for waiting for me.'
- 'Diana, I'm so happy to see you!'
- 'How are you feeling about that last meeting?'"

I said, "What else does she do that you wish all bosses knew to do?"

Diana said, "She...

- Listens to understand what I'm trying to say. She paraphrases my words to ensure she got it right.
- Treats me with dignity, like I'm an equally contributing party. She incorporates my input into her work and credits me.
- Takes into account my family obligations and trusts me to complete my tasks in a timely manner."

Rhonda demonstrates compassion for employees within their context and sets clear boundaries for success. From what Diana told me, it's clear Rhonda recognizes a cohesive culture is created one conversation at a time. Creating such bonds with employees breaks down communication gaps, encourages equitable opportunities and helps employees feel connected with the company. Not only does a trusted boss, mentor or advisor help ensure an employee feels valued and seen in their workplace, 90% of workers who have a trusted mentor report being happy in their job (Wronski, 2019).

What are the 5 C's™ of Diana's Story?

Take a few minutes to consider how the 5 C's™ apply in the case study about Diana:

- Curiosity
- Contemplation
- Courage
- Context
- Compassion

CONVERSATION PARTNER EXERCISE

You'll need your Conversation Partner to do this "One Speaker, One Listener" exercise together. With your conversation partner, take the opportunity to practice active listening. As you work toward a shared understanding with the person, keep in mind that active listening does not indicate agreement with their actions or thoughts; it only indicates compassion for them, their feelings and their experience.

This is how it works. In this activity:

1. The speaker shares their story about a current challenge in a relationship.

2. The listener hears the speaker out.

3. As the speaker is sharing, the listener labels the emotion(s) 2-7 times – whatever it takes for the speaker to feel heard.

4. After the speaker takes a breath, sounds more like themselves and drops into quiet, the listener may ask open-ended questions to gather more information about the person's experience.

5. Use Steps 2-4 as needed to get to shared understanding, then switch roles and repeat the exercise.

When you're the speaker:

- Share your story (2-3 minutes each).
- Notice your own feelings as you speak.
- Notice if you feel vulnerable speaking and recognize that vulnerability most often comes across as courage.

When you're the listener:

- Notice hidden assumptions that show up which might distract you from really listening.
- Notice your own feelings as you spot the speaker's emotion.
- Notice how you want to problem-solve (but don't problem-solve).
- Allow the speaker to finish sharing before you label their emotion.

BREATHE AND RELAX

Contemplation is a way of listening with your heart while not relying entirely on your head. Fr. Richard Rohr defines contemplation as "a long loving look" (2017). When you find yourself in your head, stuck in a loop of self-judgment, slow down. It may be counterintuitive, but take three deep breaths and feel the suffering of believing you're "not okay." Notice where you feel that suffering in your body. Then, offer a gesture of kindness and understanding to those feelings. You might hold your hands over your heart and whisper to yourself, "Be gentle."

Or, "I understand, this is hard." Notice what happens when you take a moment or minute to accept yourself as you are in all your humanity – all the broken and beautiful parts in there together.

THREE-DAY CHALLENGE

During the next three days, observe, experience and practice active listening in your organization or community. Use your head, heart and hands to reflect on and write in your journal:

Day 1: Today, look for examples of passive and active listening.

1. Where do you see active listening demonstrated and where is it missing?
2. How did active listening change the dynamic of the conversation you observed?
3. How does Minimization deter you from actively listening and accepting your own humanity just as you are?

Day 2: Today, observe how active listening makes you and others feel.

1. What are the situations where you wish someone had actively listened to you?
2. What are the situations where you inadvertently didn't listen and wish you had?
3. How does active listening change how you feel about others?

Day 3: Today, watch for times when active listening is needed individually and collectively to the benefit of your organization or community.

1. What practice or policy in your organization or community inadvertently or intentionally leaves people feeling sidelined or silenced?

2. Who can help you determine impacted stakeholders?

3. What cultural intelligence tools can you use to take a first step so that those stakeholders feel valued, heard, seen and engaged?

CONCLUSION:
GETTING TO A WIN-WIN

To prevent humiliating collisions with the universe,
I suggest we all adopt an attitude of being open to learning in
every moment of our relationships. Every interaction contains
within it the possibility of deep connection with our beloved,
with ourselves and with the cosmos. Each time we approach
a conversation with an attitude of learning, it cuts down on
friction and enhances the possibility of deep connection.

-GAY HENDRICKS

In capitalist societies, competitiveness is a cultural characteristic that, if you're not culturally aware, can get in the way of productive and genuine relationships. You can get caught up in trying to figure out who's right and who's wrong in a conversation. You can get attached to the idea that someone is a loser and someone is a winner, and you want to win.

But when one person wins, the other loses. It's their loss or ours. But if one person loses, both parties lose, actually. They lose the opportunity to build a relationship. They lose connection. Organizations and communities lose productivity and commitment.

So, how do we all win?

You know we've all really "won" when we feel compassion from and for our colleagues and clients. Like the man who realized his Confederate flag might keep him from getting to know his neighbor.

The truth is, the survival and well-being of our organizations depend on our collective well-being, not our individual power. Our collective well-being develops one culturally intelligent conversation at a time.

It is within individual conversations that you are able to pick up on patterns of how employees, customers, friends and family may feel sidelined or silenced. Like when the store manager took the time to slow down and demonstrate compassion for her younger employee and realize greater connection, commitment and productivity. This is the real power a culturally intelligent leader wields.

Your job as a culturally intelligent leader is to notice, feel and respond to systems within your organization and community that are marginalizing, silencing or excluding people. Just as the CEO discovered when he took the time to learn what was causing his employee to be late for work. It may be a lack of quality public transportation or good childcare. It could be a lack of compassion toward different viewpoints or value systems that cut off valuable innovation.

While words like compassion, feelings and belonging may resonate with you as words that should be used at home with family rather than professional life, it is the exclusion of these words in our workplace, community and greater society that marginalizes entire groups of people, minimizes important experiences we could all learn from and alienates us from innovation that moves us forward in life and business. Just imagine the opportunities for genuine connection and real engagement when you slow down and demonstrate compassion and solidarity for another person within their context. Fostering a shared understanding and trust is the means to an end for greater engagement, commitment, retention in any organization and community.

NEXT STEPS

In this book, you've learned that cultural intelligence is what enables you to successfully navigate conversations with people who are different so that you can attract, retain and engage diverse talent and reach a broader market. Within your encounters, you can notice, name and note patterns in the system that are inadvertently sidelining and silencing people in your organization and marketplace. As you and your conversation partner, along with your colleagues, learn, practice and continue to develop these skills of cultural intelligence, you'll be able to work together to address alienating corporate patterns along with those who are impacted. In cahoots, you can work shoulder-to-shoulder to create practices and policies so that everyone feels valued, heard, seen and engaged. Culturally intelligent leaders know that this cohesive culture is created and sustained one conversation at a time.

You can:

1. Take the Intercultural Development Inventory® (IDI®). [As mentioned in Chapter 3: Making the Case for Diversity.] Discover your current mindset, empower yourself with self-awareness and develop two SMART goals for culturally intelligent leadership.

2. Get one-to-one Executive Coaching. Using the tools for culturally intelligent leadership, resolve conflicts for win-win scenarios, set clear boundaries without alienating colleagues and engage stakeholders in a way that's meaningful for them in their context.

3. Grab your team, invite them to take the Dr. Amy's Workshop Series to learn together in real-time, practice the tools and craft the practices that ensure everyone feels valued, heard, seen and engaged.

ABOUT THE AUTHOR

DR. AMY NARISHKIN

Retention and engagement are at an all-time low, and leaders are finding they must create a culture of safety and belonging. With a PhD in adult education and over three decades of experience, Dr. Amy is a speaker, author and coach working with organizations and their leaders who want to be confident communicators so that they can attract and retain diverse talent. As CEO of Empowering Partners, LLC, she has worked with more than 400 leaders in China, India, Columbia, El Salvador, Venezuela, Argentina, Mexico, Nigeria, South Africa, the UK and in the U.S. to effectively increase their ability to lead, retain and engage people who have different perspectives and backgrounds. Dr. Amy is a Qualified Administrator of a globally recognized tool for measuring the ability to navigate cross-cultural conversations - the Intercultural Development Inventory® (IDI®). In program evaluations, she regularly receives over 90% "exceeds expectations" from participants. As a cross-cultural thought leader and successful entrepreneur, Dr. Amy empowers leaders to create an environment where everyone feels valued, heard, seen and engaged. To jump-start your organization's cultural intelligence and feel confident creating a cohesive culture one conversation at a time, contact Dr. Amy and read her blog: **www.EmpoweringPartners.com.**

APPENDIX

COMMUNICATION GUIDELINES

To maximize engagement in your team meetings, you can intentionally set these guidelines for speech and behavior. That way, you won't miss valuable front-line input because of one-way communication habits. Here are some guidelines you can use:

1. Affirm another's experience, whether or not your experience is the same.
2. Listen actively – hear the person out.
3. Check the impact of your words rather than explaining your intent.
4. Honor confidentiality.
5. Share airtime and let the person finish talking.
6. Speak from my own experience – use "I" statements.
7. Say "Ouch" if you've been hurt.
8. Say "Oops" if you mess up.
9. Express curiosity and wonder with gentle questions.

Steps for implementation

The leader says, "Because everyone's ideas are important to the group dynamics, we're putting in place these Communication Guidelines. These guidelines are not necessarily intuitive and may run counter-cultural so it can be uncomfortable initially. But with practice, the awkwardness will pass. As the guidelines become the new norm, the upside is everyone will feel more valued, heard, seen and engaged."

Before you start using them, take some time to review the Guidelines aloud and express appreciation as participants use them during and after the meeting. To maximize participation, start the discussion with an open-ended question, such as: "What are the needs?" or "Who does this work impact?" You might even send the question to the group ahead of time because people who are introverted, neurodivergent or part of a historically marginalized group may appreciate the opportunity to think ahead.

SELF-AWARENESS IS KEY TO A COHESIVE CULTURE

Each team member becoming more self-aware of how their thoughts, feelings, words and actions impact themselves and others is key to developing a cohesive culture at work. Cultural self-awareness is the pathway for ensuring no one feels sidelined or silenced, creating more engagement, collaboration and commitment in any organization.

Without self-awareness, there is often an:

1. Incongruence between your feelings and your non-verbal communication, and;

2. Inability to see how you're impacting others.

To develop self-awareness and close this gap between your feelings and nonverbals, consider this poem about emotion.

The root word of "Emotion" is motion.
That suggests, emotions are transitory by nature,
*   temporary visitors.*

It may sound odd, can be counter-intuitive
*   and is definitely counter-cultural...*
Our emotions are here to teach us, guide us and leave.
They don't speak English, so they come as feelings,
To be noticed and named,
To be noticed and named.

That's why the Feelings Wheel can be so helpful.
When your feelings show up, invite them to pull up
*   a chair and sit down.*
Give them a name,
Name them correctly.
Remind your feelings they are valid, even though sometimes
*   they can be a lot.*
If they're too much, speak them aloud to a trusted friend or advisor
who loves you well.

Breathe, deep and slow.

Withhold judgment.

Lean in.

Listen up.

Offer appreciation for teaching you, for guiding you.

Recognize some feelings are coming up from past harms or hurts.

Know that they often come in a bundle.

In either case, they're transitory and helpful, if you...

Slow down, sit down, let them teach you.

That's what allows them, encourages them to move on or through.

In light of the five stages of cultural intelligence,
    consider this about emotions...

To deny them is to be driven by them.

To judge them is to abandon yourself or the other.

To minimize them is to perpetuate them, which can lead to
self-denial and self-loathing.

But...

To accept them is to allow them to teach you and
    move on or through.

This is what allows you to adapt your words and actions
    to show yourself and others the genuine respect you
    and they are worthy of.

HOW TO BE AN ALLY

To benefit from having a diverse team, it's important to recognize it's not uncommon for people of the dominant culture in any community, organization or country to be culturally blind to the system and the way it affects themselves and the people from historically marginalized groups, be they women, people of color or those who are neurodivergent. To be an effective ally and lift up others' voices, you can be alert to how Minimization inadvertently infiltrates your conversations, even with the best of intentions.

To be a culturally intelligent ally:

- Listen, don't talk. Resist the temptation to jump in and speak for someone before you talk with them. Don't assume you know what they need. That would be minimization. To learn about their experience, ask, "May I ask you a question?" And, "What happened to you?"
- Focus on them, not you. It can be tempting to get people to focus on you as the advocate, but then you end up minimizing their voice. Leaders make it about the other person and step back. You might say, "Elena gave me permission to share her idea." Or, "Aaron had an insight. Would you like to share it now or in an email, Aaron?"
- Talk *with* them, not about them. Effective leaders don't guess based on appearance but find out from the source what the needs are. They notice who's not in the room and who is impacted by decisions being made. Leaders

do the rounds and walk the floor to learn first-hand. They ask, "What are the needs?" then later paraphrase what they heard and say, "Do I understand correctly? Is this what really matters to you?" [Management systems have espoused similar practices. Hewlett Packard coined the practice of "Management by Walking Around" or MBWA. In the Toyota Production System, there are the two concepts of GEMBA walks and "Go and See" or Genchi Genbutsu.]

- Learn from your mistakes. When you overstep and get called out, it's tempting to drop into silence with shame or react in anger by defending yourself. Instead, S.T.O.P. – Slow down, Take a breath, Observe your feelings and imagine how the other person feels, then Proceed with curiosity and wonder to see what you can learn about how the dominant culture impacts others. So often, it's in that moment of vulnerability that we find compassion for others and can perceive practices or policies that need to change.

- Recognize that trust is built over time. After years of being belittled under the system of minimization, people of non-dominant groups may hesitate to speak up for fear of retaliation, misrepresentation, social isolation or job loss, even when asked to speak up. You may have to listen deeply several times before a person is possibly ready to open up.

- Speak up for others. If someone says something hateful or ignorant, invite them to share what happened that made them feel the way they do. Whether or not you can imagine what happened or agree with their conclusion, you can affirm their feelings. Then you can ask if you can share your perspective.

When community members use their cultural intelligence to appreciate that everyone's experience is unique and we can all learn from one another, this is what enables us to create safe, cohesive communities and companies.

GLOSSARY

CHAPTER 1: UNDERSTANDING CULTURAL INTELLIGENCE

Cultural intelligence is the ability to appreciate another person's perspective and adapt your words and actions to demonstrate genuine respect and interest in them. Put another way, you'll be able to demonstrate meaningful compassion as you learn more about the other person's context. This is cultural intelligence in action.

5 C's™:

Curiosity is the interest, intrigue and wonder about people, places and systems that are new and different.

Contemplation is slowing down, softening our gaze to practice presence. Presence is the embodied awareness of your mental, emotional and sensory experience.

Courage is the interest, intrigue and wonder about people, places and systems that are new and different, even though it may initially feel awkward, scary or hard.

Context is the set of unique circumstances, history and cultural containers within which each of us lives, works and plays.

Compassion happens when we hold our judgment a little more lightly to make room for another's perspective and feel with them. It's then that, in solidarity, we create meaningful practices and policies that ensure each of us feels valued, heard and engaged.

CHAPTER 2: BUILDING COMMON VOCABULARY

Culture is a set of behaviors, customs, attitudes, values, beliefs and perceptions that people in a particular group have in common.

Visible culture refers to the easily observable and tangible aspects of a culture, like clothing, food, art, language, and rituals, that are readily apparent to people observing from the outside.

Invisible culture is created by a group of people in the forms of values, beliefs and perceptions that often guide a person but are not immediately apparent or tangible. People learn their values and beliefs from their families, places of worship, the media, school and work.

Dominant culture is the culture that is the most powerful, widespread or influential within a society or community where multiple cultures are present. In a society, it refers to the established language, religion, values, rituals and social customs that make it the widely considered "norm."

Non-dominant culture is a distinct group differentiated by race, religion, caste, gender, wealth, health, disability, age, appearance or orientation that coexists with but is subordinate to the dominant culture. Although not always, it is often smaller in number and is distinct from the dominant culture because of visible and invisible cultural differences. In the U.S., non-dominant cultures can be referred to as "diverse cultures," "historically-marginalized groups" or "under-represented groups."

Visible diversity is, for example, age, gender, race, physical disability, appearance and nationality.

Invisible Diversity is, for example, religion, mental and/or emotional challenges, geographic background, travel experience, education level or socio-economic status.

Belonging in a group is a feeling of acceptance, whereby group members feel seen, heard and valued by other group members and are able to provide that experience for fellow group members as well. Culturally intelligent organizations are intentional about building a culture of appreciation, belonging and connection.

CHAPTER 3: MAKING THE CASE

Intercultural mindset is a mindset that supports, allows and advocates for the expression of multiple cultural group perspectives.

Denial is little to no recognition of more complex cultural differences. It is often unintended and due to missing cultural differences of people.

Polarization is a judgmental orientation toward cultural commonalities and differences; it is a binary mindset – "us versus them."

Monocultural mindset is a mindset that supports, advocates or allows for the expression of a single cultural group perspective.

Minimization highlights cultural commonalities that can mask deeper recognition and understanding of cultural differences; it believes that focusing on commonalities is best.

Cultural assimilation is when a person or group absorbs, resembles or assumes the values, behaviors and beliefs of the dominant group, whether fully or partially. This is done inadvertently or intentionally.

Acceptance is being curious about and interested in cultural commonalities as well as differences in one's own and other cultures; it sees diversity as an asset but is unclear about how to adapt behavior to show genuine respect.

Adaptation is the ability to appreciate another cultural perspective and shift words and actions to show genuine respect within the cultural context. People who reach this stage recognize their own cultural systems of power and influences and choose to use their power to ensure each voice feels valued and engaged.

CHAPTER 4: OUTSMARTING ASSUMPTIONS

Assumption is an idea that we accept as true about a person, group or situation without any proof that it's true.

Hidden assumption (see definition of "unconscious bias" just below)

Unconscious bias or a hidden assumption occurs automatically when the brain makes fast judgments based on experiences and/or background. The fast thinking results in prejudice or unsupported judgments in favor of or against one thing, person or group as compared to another. With unconscious biases, certain people benefit, and other people do not.

Slow thinking is slowing down, taking a breath and noticing your assumptions, then proceeding with curiosity and wonder to get more information about a person or situation.

Fast thinking is instinctive, automatic, incomplete, effortless, biased and involves fallible thought fragments. This is how brains are conditioned to function reflexively, a holdover from a time when fight or flight was necessary for survival.

Stereotyping is categorizing people, groups and situations based on fast thinking and oversimplification.

Confirmation bias is the tendency to overvalue data and observations that fit with or confirm our existing beliefs.

Dunning-Kruger Effect bias is cognitive bias, where a person with a low level of knowledge in a particular subject mistakenly assesses their knowledge or ability as greater than it is.

Negativity bias is cognitive bias, where a person irrationally weighs the potential for a negative outcome as more important than that of a positive outcome.

Self-serving effect bias is cognitive bias, where a person inaccurately attributes successes to themselves and fails to accept interference by other people or situations.

The Curse of Knowledge and Hindsight biases are cognitive biases where a person assumes others know the same information and/or have the same experiences.

Optimism/Pessimism biases are cognitive biases where a person's mood or outlook inaccurately shapes their belief. If we feel good, our bias is to a positive outcome, and when we feel bad, our bias is to a negative outcome.

Backfire effect bias is a cognitive bias where a person reactively clings harder or defends a belief with more force after it has been challenged.

In-group bias is a cognitive bias where a person unfairly favors or prefers someone in their own group or someone like them over other people.

CHAPTER 5: EXPRESSING COMPASSION

Empathy is to feel with another or look from their perspective in an attempt to understand why they feel the way they do. It doesn't require that we have experienced the same situation they are going through, but it does require courage, vulnerability and active listening. Empathy helps us feel connected.

Sympathy comes from the ego. It's what we know we should do and it often involves telling others what to do or feel. Sympathy tends to make the receiver feel more alone.

Dignity is the inherent worth of every human being.

Solidarity is a demonstration of unity in thoughts, words and actions that produces a community of interest, objectives and standards.

Accountability is taking responsibility, individually and collectively, for our words and actions and their impact.

CHAPTER 6: RECOGNIZING OUR CULTURE

Cultural blindness is the belief that one's own culture and norms are universally applicable, overlooking the opportunities other cultures have to offer. This perception can be well-intentioned but is definitely flawed – limiting productivity, engagement and commitment.

Competitiveness as a cultural characteristic is a binary separation of people and groups into one winner and the rest losing or made to feel less-than.

Perfectionism as a cultural characteristic leads people and groups to be judgmental and identify what is wrong with themselves, others and situations.

Urgency as a cultural characteristic is when time is viewed as linear rather than flexible; faster is better.

Task-oriented as a cultural characteristic is the ability to complete tasks reliably in a timely fashion. It can become a problem when completing a task is prioritized over the needs or feelings of the people involved.

Heart trust arises from emotional feelings of connection through talking, laughing and experiencing together. From shared experience, we reach a level of comfort together that leads to vulnerability, closeness, empathy and friendship. This type of trust is relationally based on connected, shared experiences.

Head trust arises more from an intellectual trust or confidence in someone's skills and reliability. We work together and rely on one another to complete tasks, follow directions and check in when help is needed. This type of trust is more transactional, or cognitively based, relying on repeated actions and less on emotional connection.

CHAPTER 7: LISTENING TO UNDERSTAND

Passive listening is allowing someone to speak without interrupting; not doing anything else at the same time, and yet not really paying attention to what's being said.

Active Listening is listening and responding (with facial expression, body language and sounds such as "hmm" or "ah") while paying close attention to the speaker. This is followed by paraphrasing the content and/or feeling of what was said after the speaker finishes speaking as a technique to help the listener and speaker arrive at a mutual understanding.

Paraphrasing is using your own words to say back what you heard the speaker said and the feeling they expressed to ensure a shared understanding.

Performance Improvement Plan (PIP) is a formal, structured process used by employers to address employee under-performance, outlining specific areas for improvement, setting achievable goals, and providing a time frame for achieving those goals, with clear consequences for failure to meet expectations.

REFERENCES

Alexander, M. (2010) The New Jim Crow. New York: The New Press.

Banaji, M. & Greenwald, A. (2013) Blindspot: Hidden Biases of Good People. New York: Delacorte Press.

Brown, B. (2012) Daring Greatly. New York: Avery Books.

Calvin, C (Jan 9, 2023) How many workers feel undervalued? Almost half, Workhuman suggests. HR Dive: https://www.hrdive.com/news/workers-feel-undervalued-workhuman/639999/

Cloud, H. (2013) Boundaries for Leaders. New York: Harper-Collins.

Eisenstein, C. (Nov 2016) The Election: Of Hate, Grief, and a New Story, https://charleseisenstein.org/essays/hategriefandanewstory/

Campt, D. (2018) The White Ally Toolkit Workbook

Chemaly, S. (2018) Rage Becomes Her. New York: Atria Books.

Grant, A. (2017) Originals: How Non-Conformists Move the World. New York: Penguin Books.

Hammer, M. (2011). *Additional cross-cultural validity testing of the Intercultural Development International Journal of Intercultural Relations, 35, 474-487,* https://idiinventory.com/wp-content/uploads/2014/02/IDI-Validation-article-2011.pdf

Hammer, M. (2016) *Intercultural Development Inventory Resource Guide. Olney, MD: IDI, LLC.*

Henricks, G. (2009) *The Big Leap. New York: Harper Collins Publishers.*

Hofstede, G., Hofstede, G. J., Minkov, M. (2010) *Cultures and Organizations: Software of the Mind. New York: McGraw Hill.*

Hunt, V., Prince, S., Dixon-Fyle, S., & Yee, L. (2018) *Delivering Through Diversity. McKinsey & Co.*

Kahneman, D (2011) *Thinking, Fast and Slow. New York: Penguin Books.*

Lupton, R. (1989) *Theirs is the Kingdom, San Francisco: Harper.*

Maznevski, M. & DiStefano, J. (Oct 2012) *Creating Value with Diverse Teams in Global Management, Organizational Dynamics, 29(1):45-63.*

Meyer, E (2014) *The Culture Map, New York: Public Affairs Publishing.*

Norlander, P., Does, S., & Shih, M., (2019) Deprivation at work: The Racial Gap Between White and Non-White Americans' Quality of Work Life, Referenced as ongoing research in Peter Norlander's faculty profile at Loyola University Chicago's Quinlan School of Business.

Rohr, R. (2017) Daily meditations. https://cac.org/daily-meditations/contemplative-christianity-great-tradition-2017-01-19/

Van Edwards, V. (2018) Captivate. New York: Penguin.

Voss, C. (2016) Never Split the Difference. New York: Harper-Collins.

Wronski, L (July 16, 2019) CNBC: Nine in 10 workers who have a career mentor say they are happy in their jobs. https://www.cnbc.com/2019/07/16/nine-in-10-workers-who-have-a-mentor-say-they-are-happy-in-their-jobs.html

ACKNOWLEDGMENTS

I am forever grateful for:

My husband, Cyril Narishkin, whose integrity, wisdom and compassion are a beacon for me, our family and our community. With his international perspective, he encourages all those he encounters to consider the impact of their actions on those around them and holds us all accountable with love. He has been my biggest cheerleader as I continue to learn and grow.

My four adult children, Tally Narishkin, Abby Narishkin, Christopher Narishkin and Chloe Narishkin, who have big hearts for people, have integrated cultural intelligence into their work and relationships and make their parents proud every day.

My sister, Anne Collier, for sharing her wisdom and editing expertise, and holding me lovingly accountable for compassion and clarity.

My pastor, Dr. Julius Sims, and his wife, Cathy Sims, for being willing to open up their minds, hearts and church to this work. They and their congregation embraced me and my family and grew along with us. I've been blessed with their unconditional love, gentle nudges to be more aware of my impact in the community and extraordinary encouragement to be both content and keep on going and growing.

My thought partner, Catherine Hunter, for listening deeply and asking just the right reflective questions so that I and the people we serve feel valued, seen and heard.

My mentor, Robin Radford, for holding my feet to the fire with great love and helping me see, appreciate and hurt for people with experiences different from my own.

My spiritual director, Wendy Everts, who helps me deepen my relationship within, with others and with the divine. Through deep listening and compassion, she helps me recognize my humanity – all the beautiful and messy parts in there together – so that I can contribute in some small way to the world's wellbeing one moment at a time.

My friends, NancyDee MacFarland, Kim St. Clair, Darlene Caldwell, Kit McGrath, Jonathan Victorian, Margarita Zapiain Bazdresch, Beth Redmond-Jones, Bettie Rooks, Alvaro Nieva, Ron Radford and Piotr Perczynski for listening, teaching and cheerleading as I learn and grow.

My publishing team, Cathy Davis, Missy Asikainen and Kim Fletcher, for their wisdom, grace, tenacity and creativity as they helped me bring the book to fruition.

My clients, who have big hearts and open minds. Thank you for your willingness to grow and learn along with me. Because you prioritize your people – you and your organization experience evermore engagement, collaboration and commitment. You are an extraordinary leader.

My readers, who are courageous and compassionate. I appreciate how you send me notes and articles of encouragement to help me keep on going. Thank you for introducing me to leaders who want to and are ready to do this work. I love how you are working to upend the polarization in your organization and society as a whole. I appreciate how you strive to take a deep breath before you respond and help to create a more compassionate community where everyone feels valued, heard, seen and engaged. You are a compassionate trailblazer.